The Picklin' Parson's Cookbook

THE PICKLIN' PARSON'S COOKBOOK
...and Stories to Ponder When Uncle Sam's in a Pickle

Library of Congress Cataloging-in-Publication Data

Copeland, Stanley R., 1959
The Picklin' Parson's Cookbook...and Stories to Ponder When Uncle Sam's in a Pickle

Stillwater Market Farm Productions   stillwatermarket.farm

ISBN 9780578798806

All scripture quotations unless noted otherwise are taken from The Message Bible authored by Eugene Peterson.
Chandler: Its History and People, Joy Clark, Margaret Cade John L. Clark Editors Commemorating the Centennial of Chandler, Texas—1880-1980, copyright 1981
Way Back When Stories of Chandler's Past, Jim Sidney Powell author, copyright 2009
Favorite Recipes 1963 W.S.C.S., Chandler Methodist Church, Chandler, Texas
Prize Recipes of Chandler, Chandler Volunteer Fire Department, Chandler, Texas
Our Daily Bread Women's *Our Common Table*, 2019 Wesley Prep, Café Momentum, Bonton Farms

MANUFACTURED IN THE UNITED STATES OF AMERICA

The Picklin' Parson's Cookbook

TABLE of CONTENTS

The Picklin' Parson's Cookbook

The Picklin' Parson's Cookbook

The Picklin' Parson's Cookbook

THE PICKLIN' PARSON'S COOKBOOK

...And Stories to Ponder When Uncle Sam's in a Pickle

Stanley R. Copeland

Foreword by

Tammy B. Copeland

(The Parson's Spouse)

The Picklin' Parson's Cookbook

AN OPENING WORD
By Tammy Barnes Copeland

I've heard people say through the years that being a pastor's wife must be pretty challenging. I have always thought that it really isn't terribly challenging—that is, until the parson, my hubby, started pickling and canning. Stan came by his allure to the kitchen honestly from the way he grew up around so many of his cooking grandparents and the extended family scene in Chandler, Texas. It's as if the attraction to cooking is in his genes. I will say he's getting pretty good at pickling and canning. However, he is slower to improve on his mess-cleaning-up skills, which still makes for a challenge. It put him in a pickle or two with me.

In 2021 we will have been married for 40 years, and our life together is full of fun memories from the kitchen. I remember shortly after we were married, we moved to Kansas City where Stan attended seminary at St. Paul School of Theology. We were young—22 and 20. We set up house in a 300 sq. ft. campus apartment on the third floor. We hauled all our belongings up three flights of stairs, including a 3-foot by 3-foot box freezer—one of our first purchases. It was full of catfish, purple hull peas and blackberries. If that's not "country boy come to town," I don't know what is.

We had gotten an electric ice cream maker and a blender as wedding gifts. Stan decided to transform his Grandmother Mersie Reagan's vanilla ice cream recipe into blackberry ice cream by simply adding the berries. He blended the ice cream mixture and blackberries together, which turned the concoction into a Barney-the-Dinosaur purple color. It did freeze, and was ice cream alright, but there was a seed-crunch with every unattractive purple bite. I'll put it this way, there is a reason Blue Bell doesn't have blackberry ice cream as a choice.

From that little apartment in Kansas City to our first little parsonage in Henderson, Texas, we have found cooking in our kitchens as places to create and bring people together around good

The Picklin' Parson's Cookbook

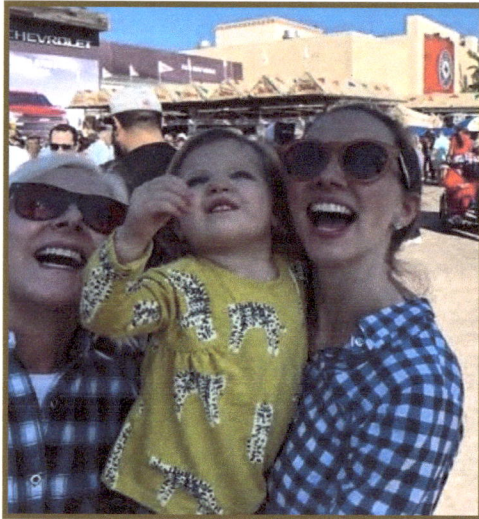

food. I remember the first parsonage we had in Houston. The kitchen had a self-cleaning oven, which was a real deal. Ever since my life partner, the parson, started pickling and canning, I have longed for a self-cleaning kitchen. I've trained him to do many things through the years, but I still have work to do. Maybe with the 40th anniversary year coming, and the "40" number being "holy" and all, my prayers will be answered, and my parson husband will meet my cleaning standards. If only I can get him over his fear of opening the dishwasher and putting the dirty dishes and utensils in it.

I will say that I really do enjoy him sharing his pickles and jams with our granddaughter, Claire Marie "Claire Bear" Copeland. She does love his sweet pickles by way of his Mawmaw Ellis. It is cool to think that these Virginia Sweet Chunk Pickles are at least a seventh-generation recipe to her and possibly 10 generations, since Mawmaw's roots are actually by way of Virginia, three generations prior to her being born in East Texas. Claire Bear also loves books and stories and one day, I can see us reading her Pop's stories in the cookbook. Soon, she'll be reading them herself. Whether Claire Bear joins her "Pop" in his pickling and canning ventures is yet to be seen. I will do my best to instill good kitchen etiquette and cleaning habits with our granddaughter who will be a "big sister" before you read this cookbook.

All kidding aside, the recipes are fun to try out, and the stories will make you laugh. Some will even bring a tear to your eye. Stan's concoctions have won ribbons at the State Fair of Texas in Dallas and the East Texas State Fair in Tyler. He even got me in on the canning, and together, we won six ribbons at the State Fair of Texas this year. Last year he entered his first picklin' and canning creations in the two Texas state fairs, so his two years of prizes now total thirteen.

He is most excited however, about the cookbook being a gift to his hometown of Chandler for its 140th anniversary. There is some Chandler history told in his own unique way. And the reader will see that he couldn't help but preach a bit. He has always been committed to the "Methodist thing" of the Holy Spirit moving us toward being "perfected in love" and "God's kingdom coming on earth as it is in heaven." This passion has kept this parson busy spinning tales, sharing scripture and sermonizing to raise our consciousness to Christian values, social justice, how we treat each other as sisters and brothers and an undeniable, amazing grace. I think you will enjoy this "more than a cookbook."

The Picklin' Parson's Cookbook

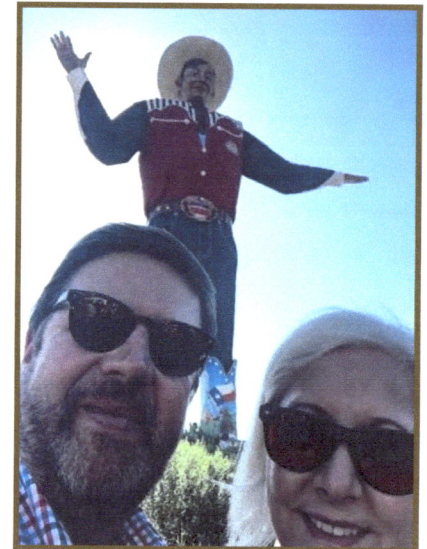

I still enjoy my parson, who's been my partner for four decades, and he still makes me laugh. Like most good marriages that last decades, we have had high-highs and low-lows. Through it all, the constants have been having a wonderful family, friends, community, and congregations. We have so much to be thankful for. I am thankful that Stan's style of preaching and writing is so story-driven, and therefore, much of our time together has been written down as the "good stuff" that makes for sermons and now, even a cookbook. I better go check the kitchen; I hear him clanking around in there right now.

Love God, your God, with your whole heart: love him with all that's in you, love him with all you've got! Write these commandments that I've given you today on your hearts. Get them inside of you and then get them inside your children. Deuteronomy 6:5-7

Happy the Home When God Is There

1. Hap - py the home when God is there,
and love fills ev - ery breast;
when one their wish, and
one their prayer, and one their heaven - ly rest.

2. Hap - py the home where Je - sus' name
is sweet to ev - ery ear;
where chil - dren ear - ly
speak his fame, and pa - rents hold him dear.

3. Hap - py the home where prayer is heard,
and praise is wont to rise;
where pa - rents love the
sa - cred Word and all its wis - dom prize.

4. Lord, let us in our homes a - gree
this bles - sed peace to gain;
u - nite our hearts in
love to thee, and love to all will reign

The Picklin' Parson's Cookbook

Dedicated in Memory
of
Megan Elizabeth McGill Dobrinski

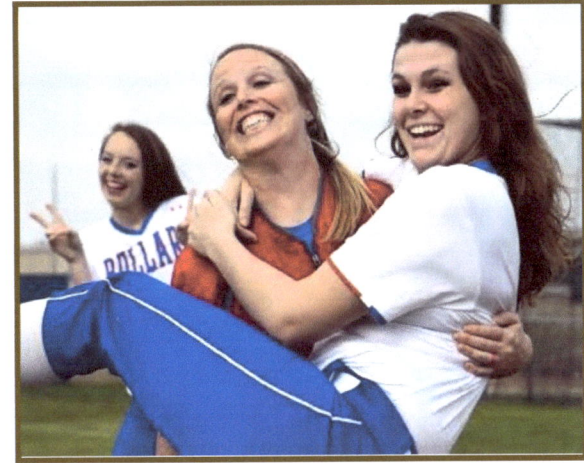

If you didn't know my niece, Megan, I'm truly sorry. She was a joy and a blessing to many, and she would have been to you. If you did know her, you knew "Smiley's" passion for faith, family, community and team. She was a Daughter, Sister, Granddaughter, Niece, Cousin, Wife, Mom, Friend, and Coach. Those were her roles in life that she played with passion and joy. Her beautiful face was always radiant with a smile that she was known for. When you saw her smiling face, it made you want to smile back and attracted you to her like a magnetic force.

Her athletic ability was only topped by her incredible people skills and relational nature which made her a great coach. We still miss her every day since she outran us to heaven on August 14, 2019. We will never forget her, and slowly but surely, our memories are bringing to bear the joy of the blessing of her life rather than the overwhelming grief of our incredible loss.

The Reverend Dr. John Claypool wrote about his daughter Laura Lou who died from leukemia at the age of 10 years old. His words in the little book, *Tracks of a Fellow Struggler* have become like a mantra to me regarding Megan. The third sermon or chapter was entitled, "Life is a Gift." The message of this chapter was the great takeaway of the entire book. Claypool spoke of "three routes." Two of the routes he described as dead ends, and one seemed quite promising. The first route was described as the "road of unquestionable resignation." He ultimately

The Picklin' Parson's Cookbook

asked the question, "Where, then, did we Christians ever get the notion that we must not question God or that we have no right to pour out our souls to God and ask, 'Why?'" He responded, "I honor God by continuing to ask, and seek and knock, rather than resign myself like a leaf on a rock." He then shared a word a fellow pastor, Dr. Carlyle Marney, had shared with him. Marney said, "I fall back on the notion that God has a lot to account for." And Claypool said, "I believe God will be able to give an accounting when all of the facts are in."

The second dead end route was the one of "the road of total intellectual understanding." He said though he was tempted to conclude, "A long time ago I decided that you do not solve all of the intellectual problems by concluding that everything is absurd." Claypool quotes another fellow struggler named Dr. George Buttrick, "Life is essentially a series of events to be born and lived through, rather than intellectual riddles to be played with and solved." We cannot live as if the darkness swallows up the light when we are people who "see in a glass dimly" and only "know in part."

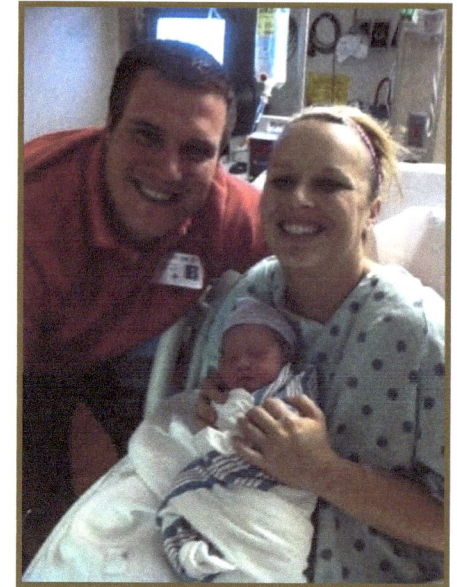

This parson's parson finally said, "Everywhere I am, I am surrounded by reminders of her—things we did together, things she did, things she loved. And in the presence of these reminders, I have two alternatives. I can dwell on the fact that she was taken away, and dissolve in remorse that all of this is gone forever. Or, focusing on the wonder that she was ever given at all, I can resolve to be grateful that we shared life, even for an all-too-short ten years. The way of gratitude does not alleviate the pain, but it somehow puts light around the darkness, and creates strength to begin to move on."

When Megan was born, I had six months prior been diagnosed with leukemia that was expected to be terminal within three years. There was no treatment for a cure at the time for the kind of leukemia I had contracted. The disease entailed a genetic mutation and always progressed to an untreatable stage. We were in Houston where I was working and being treated for the cancer. Therefore, Megan's early few years are more of a blur to me, but when I started coming out of my fog what a delight it was to see her grow into the joyous, full-of-life child, youth and then young adult that she became. I have my own questions for God to which I know the Great Healer will be able to account for. My questions are not driven by doubt, rather they are about a need for personal peace, regarding why young people acquire cancer, and some succumb to it and others survive its death grip.

The Picklin' Parson's Cookbook

My mentor Bill Hinson's words always ring in my ears, "I pray to a God who heals. Some of us may be healed miraculously and will have to find out what really happened when we get to heaven. Some of us may be healed like the Apostle Paul who prayed for the 'thorn' in his flesh to be removed and it wasn't, yet he could say, 'God's grace is sufficient to supply all my needs.' And ALL of us are healed on the other side of the Jordan in that land that knows no night, where there is no more weeping and pain. The land that is eternal in the heavens." Sweet Megan has her place there.

I don't know when Megan grew up and into that rite of passage that had her bringing a dish to family gatherings, but it happened. She always brought the same dish — her family's famous Pink Salad. It was such a perfect dish from one who was not particularly a "cook." The Pink Salad was not so delicious as it was a dish that took us all to a happy place. Oddly, it just looked like it was smiling — like Megan, and we all got a dab just to taste a bit of the joy stirred into it.

This cookbook in Megan's memory is meant to first bring "joy" through sharing faith and stories, community and family, photos and recipes. I hope it makes you smile and increases our thankfulness. I delight in the thought of her bringing in the Pink Salad.

> Go home and prepare a feast, holiday food and drink; and share it with those who don't have anything: This day is holy to God. Don't feel bad. The joy of God is your strength! Nehemiah 8:10

The Picklin' Parson's Cookbook

MEGAN'S PINK SALAD

Ingredients

- 1 large c. of crushed pineapple
- 1 small box of strawberry Jell-O
- 1 container of small curd cottage cheese
- 1 large container of Cool Whip
- ½ c. of finely chopped pecans

Reading, Cooking & Presenting

Heat pineapple over medium heat until boiling and add the Jell-O to the pineapple. Stir until it is dissolved. Remove the mixture from the burner and let it cool. Add cottage cheese, Cool Whip, and pecans, and don't forget the joy. Put in the refrigerator to let set and chill. Take it to the family gathering with a big smile on your face and watch 'em dig in.

The Picklin' Parson's Cookbook

Dedicated in Honor
of
Martha "Moppie" &
Don "Poppie" Copeland

Everybody in my little hometown of Chandler knows my parents by the names "Moppie" and "Poppie." They have lived there all of their lives, except for the two years when they moved to Austin to complete their education and graduate as forever UT Longhorns. They also lived for eighteen months in another little East Texas town called Troup. My sister Jill and I know them as Mamma and Daddy, but the grandchildren—Zachary, Megan, Morgan and Emily—changed all of that forever with the "Moppie" and "Poppie" enduring brand. Now their six great-grandchildren—Brycen, Ella, Davis, Claire, Lily (and one more on the way in December that we already count) will add to the love of these two and the enduring qualities of their names.

Dad was a pharmacist in Chandler for 50 years, and his father before him had the drug store in town. My sweet sister Jill now has the store and carries on the family pharmacy tradition. I might have gone the druggist route if God hadn't seen my chemistry grades and called me to preach.

Mom received a degree in home economics from the University of Texas and was a teacher in this discipline. She has always been a super mom, wonderful homemaker and great cook. She hails from a cooking family. Her mother—our grandmother Mersie—was one of the best cooks I have ever known, and Moppie didn't fall far from the tree. One recipe she was known for in her later years was her Friendship Bread that was made from a starter. A loaf would be shared with every visitor that came to the First United Methodist Church in Chandler, Texas.

The Picklin' Parson's Cookbook

We grew up in town, in a house my parents lived in for more than four decades. Dad's mother inherited the "farm," as we call it, from her mother Nana in the 1950s. Dad was given the farm before his mother—our Gran—died. In 2008, this beloved couple built a beautiful home on the property with its ponds, meadows, and an old barn on the hill. On August 12, 2017—the night of their youngest granddaughter Emily's (our daughter's) wedding—their house burned to the ground. They were in Dallas with all of our family when lightning struck the house, and all was lost. Everything material was lost, but the love remained. And on the strength of that love and "the peace of God, which passeth all understanding," these two in their eighth decade of life were given the wherewithal to rebuild right back on the spot where the beautiful first house stood. We all pitched in, as did the community and church, on many levels. Our son—their oldest grandchild, Zachary Barnes Copeland, who is an architect—designed their new home where they will live out their days.

Parkinson's disease has pretty much taken away Moppie's cooking days, but that doesn't mean she can't still coach the cook and share the family folklore. Poppie samples the goodies, and sometimes offers his classic remark as "Ol' Don"—who takes great pride in intentionally being grammatically incorrect, though he knows better—"That's the best I've ever ate."

Moppie and Poppie love their hometown of Chandler, and they love their home church. I am definitely biased, but when I think of my upbringing and the characters who made up the membership of the church, I do agree that it is one of the great congregations of all time. Moppie was about making every visitor to their church feel welcome. She was the consummate "friendship evangelist." In fact, she won the coveted Texas Conference of the United Methodist Church Harry Denman Evangelism Award in the 1980s. This award honors those whose ministry of evangelism consistently brings people into a life-transforming relationship with Jesus Christ. The framed certificate of the award was lost to the fire, but nothing could take from her the "friendship evangelism" spirit that she will always possess. What was her mark, her mantra, her calling card? It was Friendship Bread. She loved to deliver those loaves—with a smile of course—and an invitation to return next Sunday.

The Picklin' Parson's Cookbook

These two have blessed me with an upbringing with the values of Christian faith, the gift of family, love for community, the ability to spin a story, the valuing of photos, and a sharing of family recipes. Moppie and Poppie feel the love that so many share, and I—along with my family—are blessed admirers of these two. This cookbook, as a tribute to my parents, is also meant to share blessings from our family to the reader. May God bless you, as Poppie would say, "Real good."

The Picklin' Parson's Cookbook

MOM'S FRIENDSHIP BREAD

Starter Ingredients

- ½ c. warm water (110 degrees)
- 1 package dry yeast (instant yeast will work as well)
- 3 cups all-purpose flour
- 3 cups granulated sugar
- 3 cups of milk (2% or higher fat content)

Creating the Starter

Pour the warm water into a small glass bowl. Sprinkle the yeast over the water, and let it stand for 7 or 8 minutes to allow it to dissolve. In a larger bowl—don't use metal bowls or utensils for sourdough—mix together 1 cup of flour and 1 cup sugar with a wooden spoon. Stir in 1 cup milk and then the yeast mixture. Cover loosely with plastic wrap and allow it to stand until bubbly. Once the mixture is bubbly, pour it into a gallon-sized zippered plastic bag and seal it. Do not refrigerate. Allow the sourdough mixture to sit out at room temperature.

Day 2—Mash the bag
Day 3—Mash the bag
Day 4—Mash the bag
Day 5—Mash the bag
Day 6—Add 1 cup of flour, sugar and milk
Day 7—Mash the bag
Day 8—Mash the bag
Day 9—Mash the bag
Day 10—Pour the mixture into a bowl. Add 1 cup each of flour, granulated sugar and milk. Mix well with a wooden spoon. Divide out 1 cup portions for the starter, placing each one-cup portion in separate zippered plastic gallon bags. Seal the bags and give the starter away to friends, along with the instructions, keeping one for yourself if desired. The starter then goes back to Day 1.

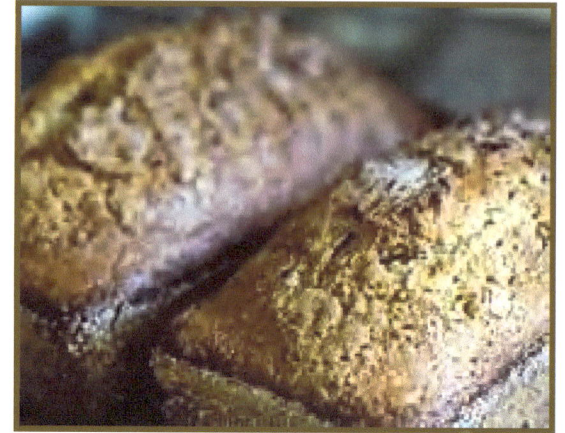

The Picklin' Parson's Cookbook

Ingredients

- 1 c. pecan oil (or other oil of choice)
- 3 large eggs
- ½ c. milk
- ½ vanilla bean paste (any vanilla will work)
- 1 c. granulated sugar
- 2 c. flour
- ½ tsp. salt
- ½ tsp. baking soda
- 1 ½ tsp. baking powder
- 2 tsp. cinnamon
- 2 smaller boxes vanilla pudding
- 1 c. chopped pecans
- 1 c. starter

Making & Baking

Create the cinnamon and sugar mixture by mixing ½ cup of sugar and 1 ½ teaspoons of cinnamon in a small bowl and set aside to use later. Preheat the oven to 325 degrees. Combine all the remaining ingredients in a large bowl and mix well. Spray two loaf pans with Pam, or any non-stick cooking spray. Dust the greased pans with the sugar and cinnamon mixture. Pour the batter equally into the pans and sprinkle the remaining sugar and cinnamon mixture over the top. Bake for one hour or until the toothpick inserted in the middle of the loaf comes out clean without any crumbs. Cool the bread until the loaves loosen evenly from the pan, and turn the pan over onto a serving dish.

> Jesus said, "I am the Bread of Life. The person who aligns with me hungers no more and thirsts no more, ever."
> John 6:35

The Picklin' Parson's Cookbook

Others

Charles D. Meigs, 1917   Elizabeth McE. Shields

1. Lord, help me live from day to day In such a self-for-
get - ful way That e - ven when I kneel to pray My
prayer shall be for— O-thers.

2. Help me in all the work I do To ev - er be sincere and true And know that all I'd do for You Must
needs be done for— O-thers. O-thers. Lord, yes o-thers, Let this my mot-to
be. Help me to live for o-thers, That I may live like Thee.

3. Let "Self" be cru - ci - fied and slain And bur - ied deep; and
all in vain May ef - forts be to rise a - gain. Unless to live for— O-thers.

4. And when my work on earth is done, And my new work in
Heav - 'n's be - gun, May I forget the crown I've won. While
think - ing still of— O-thers.

The Picklin' Parson's Cookbook

A Tribute of Thankfulness
to
Lola Bell Ray Dewberry

When one starts looking back and counting the blessings of life—gifts from God, one's heart must be full to overflowing with thankfulness. Such is the case when I count the blessing of experiencing life with Lola Bell Ray Dewberry. She was an influential, quiet, strong, and kind presence in my life. Lola Bell was present in my life growing up and in several of our sacred family homes. In Chandler, Lola Bell did domestic work—cleaning and cooking. My greatest thankfulness is that she also babysat little children, at least she did my sister and me. I write this tribute quite aware of my own privilege being white in our great nation and have witnessed some of the innate challenges of those born Black in our "liberty and justice for all" country. I am thankful for this lady of darker hue who loved so completely, and it was a gift to love her.

Lola Bell was born on March 11, 1923, about twenty-five miles from Chandler, Texas. Her Texas roots went back to her great-great grandfather who owned a farm in Chandler. And when Lola Bell spoke of her great-great grandfather, the word "owned"—in reference to their farm—speaks volumes of his farming ability, financial stability and her family pride. His land ownership would have had to go back to the days just after the Civil War, and before the railroad came through Mr. Chandler's land that birthed the new town in 1880. From slave to farm ownership was no doubt the toughest of all roads in the deep South, even in Texas. White settlers fleeing the deep South after the war was common. The black families that also traveled west, traversing the same rivers and woods, did so for the same primary reason—hoping for a more prosperous future.

Lola Bell was a person of strong faith that saw her through some very tough times. There is no question that growing up Black in East Texas had its own challenges to her that were driven by racism, and early deaths of family members and a house fire added to her mountains to climb. Her father died when she was young, yet she graduated from the segregated Central High School in Troup, Texas. Her husband, Frank, died after they were married just 17 years, yet she kept making a living and even cared for her grandmother Mary and mother Tiny who came to live with her.

The Picklin' Parson's Cookbook

It was Frank who brought Lola Bell back to her ancestral roots in Chandler when they married on August 14, 1948. Frank had a house in Chandler that in 1950 burned to the ground. Lola Bell reported in the little book *Chandler: Its History and People 1880-1980*, "In 1950 our house burned to the ground, and the people were so very good to us. We were able to build a new house shortly afterward." When Frank died in 1967, Lola Bell — who was 44 years old at the time — worked domestic jobs for white people in Chandler. Her employers were working people, but needed and could afford her assistance. Lola Bell worked for my maternal and paternal grandparents, and my parents as well.

Lola Bell was probably very good at all of her work, and I can attest to her wonderful cooking at my Copeland grandparents' house. I can see Lola Bell and Gran, big-hip to big-hip in the small kitchen, whipping up wonderful country meals for us to enjoy. I remember coming to Gran's house after school in the fall of the year and seeing the two of them canning pear honey or pear mincemeat. It was interesting to see all the quaint jars and the big black pot full of boiling water to seal the pear delicacies. I know this is a pickling and canning cookbook, but I must admit my favorite Lola Bell creations were her pies—especially her blackberry cobbler. My favorite of her cobblers was made most of the time out of wild black dewberries that were indigenous to our home area. Lola Bell was such a good cobbler cook that I imagined the "berry" was named after her—dewberry.

One of the heartaches of Lola Bell's life was that she and Frank could not have children. Perhaps that is why she seemed to treat us like cherished gifts of her own. For us, she had so much kindness, gentle-firmness, and love. I can still hear her calling me with affection with a sweet smile on her full, beautiful, dark face, "Mr. Stan," which usually came with a needed correction. I didn't think about it at the time, but it's entered my mind plenty since then, "Why would a woman a dozen years older than my parents call me "Mr. Stan?" No doubt there would be some cultural reasons that are sad for me to ponder; there was definitely a psychological backdrop to her choice of words. With her voice and chosen labels, she could make a little boy feel like he was growing up, even while still sitting in her ample lap being rocked to sleep. Little ones were ALL precious in her sight.

The Picklin' Parson's Cookbook

To be in Lola's lap in my grandmother's rocking chair as a child, was as close to the lap of God as one could come. I remember one day as a little boy being rocked by her as she hummed the familiar-to-both-of-us hymns of faith. Before I did go to sleep in her arms one common day, I asked her, "Lola Bell, why are you black?" I will never forget her answer, though I was a little boy. She told me a story, "Mr. Stan, once upon a time, God created a beautiful flower garden. There were all kinds of plants and animals and birds in the garden. There was a pond full of fish—goldfish, catfish with long whiskers, goggle-eyed fish, but the most beautiful creations in the garden were the flowers. There were little white flowers, bright yellow flowers, gorgeous red flowers, chocolate-colored brown flowers and black flowers that were as shiny as piano keys. And all those flowers together—as different as they were—made the garden beautiful. So, God decided when he made the earth to make people take care of the garden. He decided to make people like flowers—all different kinds and all different colors, and together they are beautiful. Ain't God good, Mr. Stan?" Today I would say as I do with my congregation every Sunday, "God is good all the time, and all the time God is good."

I remember the last time I saw Lola Bell. She was in her humble house in her bed in great pain, as she was dying with pancreatic cancer. The house was very warm; no, it was hot, but she was covered up with handmade quilts. She was a mere shadow of her once sturdy self. We talked briefly, but I didn't really know what to say. I had been diagnosed with terminal cancer just months prior. I hugged her and kissed her once full cheek that was drawn and dry. She said, "I love you Stan." There was no prefix "Mr." And I said with teary eyes, "And I love you too Lola Bell."

My Dad, who was a pharmacist, recently told me that he called her doctor during that time and asked him to give her something strong for pain, because her pain was unbearable. He reported that her doctor said, "I'm not about to send a narcotic prescription into 'that neighborhood.'" After her death, Dad conveyed the story to another well-known and respected surgeon. This surgeon said, "Don, you should have called me. I would have written the prescription in a New York minute, and done anything I could. She was a saint." This, of course, was the sentiment held by many. She died and was buried in the Black cemetery a mile away from the cemetery where all the White people are buried in town. This is just the way things were done for decades and are still done today. Still, Lola Bell wrote for the book about our town's people and history, *I love Chandler, and I wouldn't stay anywhere else.* And thank God that she stayed.

The Picklin' Parson's Cookbook

This is a cookbook, right? So, let me say, cooking, pickling, and canning—the kind I was exposed to growing up—was colorful. I say that it was influenced by people like Lola Bell who knew by heart the ways of the kitchen. And I know the family recipes passed down through the years were influenced by people of different and beautiful hues. This cookbook comes to be in a year, 2020, with racial divides and strife being accentuated throughout all the land.

I can pray for healing in our land, but for ME,... me,... for me, I choose to start with ownership of my privilege, which I believe gave me a "leg up," a "head start" on so many levels in contrast to the experience of others of color. I never once remember calling Lola Bell "Mrs. Dewberry," which would have been a parental mandate regarding my speech to, and of, other white elders in my hometown. For me, my statement acknowledging privilege is liberating and redemptive. This confession reminds me of my forgiving and loving God.

Others can assess for themselves the harsher realities of homogenous lifestyles and segregated living, which is not my place. And I know you will allow me to deal with my own racist tendency by asking God to perfect me in love, His love; just as it appeared God had done in Lola Bell's life.

I hope we can all agree that cooking, canning, and pickling can bring hearts together, and all of us are committed to be more about the dream of equality and justice for all. I choose to also be thankful for the experiences that I know are blessings from God, who came from saintly people like Lola Bell Ray Dewberry. To say Lola Bell was without sin would be to dehumanize her, for "all have sinned and fallen short." Lola Bell was simply one of the godliest people I've ever known and that IS the testimony of my heart.

> **In Christ's family there can be no division into Jew and non-Jew, slave and free, male and female. Among us you are all equal. That is, we are all in a common relationship with Jesus Christ. Galatians 3:28**

The Picklin' Parson's Cookbook

Lola Bell's Simple Pie Pastry

This recipe appeared in the cookbook, *Favorite Recipes 1963, Women's Society of Christian Service, Chandler Methodist Church*, Chandler, Texas.

Ingredients

- 4 . flour
- 2 c. shortening
- 1 Tbsp. salt
- 1 c. water (ice cold water is the best)

Creating the Crust

Blend the flour and the salt together. Cut in shortening with two butter knives until crumbly. Gradually add water while tossing the dough with a fork until it holds together. Divide the dough into six equal portions, and put wax paper between each portion. Put the dough in the refrigerator for one hour. Roll out each portion of dough to ¼ inch thick on a flour dusted surface. Roll out one portion and make 1 ½ inch pastry strips. Put the pastry in pie plates or cobbler dishes. Makes five or six pies.

Lola Bell's Dewberry Cobbler

Combine 5 cups of berries and 2 cups of sugar with one stick of butter. Spoon the berries evenly into the prepared dish with the bottom and sides lined with pastry. Place the pastry strips over the top and bake the cobbler at 450° for 20 minutes. Reduce the temperature to 350° and bake the cobbler for 15 more minutes or until it is golden brown.

The Picklin' Parson's Cookbook

MORE THAN A COOKBOOK

> "GOD is about to bring you into a good land, a land with brooks and rivers, springs and lakes, streams out of the hills and through the valleys. It's a land of wheat and barley, of vines and figs and pomegranates, of olives, oil, and honey. It's land where you'll never go hungry—always food on the table and a roof over your head."
> Deuteronomy 8:7-8

Did you know that God drinks coffee? I know this as reality because God drinks "joe" with me as I wake to write in the early mornings. And I believe if I were a hot tea sipper, the Creator of the Universe would be sipping with me and eating Mama Copeland Tea Cakes. With that credo established, let me say that this cookbook was created to share recipes, but much more. This cookbook came together with lots of coffee and the presence and peace of the living Lord whom I consult daily. Sometimes I would ask God about the cookbook, "Should I put it in?" Sometimes I got a Holy Spirit "thumbs up" and other times a clear "thumbs down."

The picklin' and cannin' cookbook comes to you from me as an offering of faith, family, community, stories, photos, and yes, recipes. Okay, there are a few preaching inserts as well. It is hard to separate into neat categories my experience of faith, family, and community, for they are jumbled together. This jumbled experience has been truly sweet for the most part—full of lessons of life, and I savor it more and more, the older I grow.

This cookbook is an attempt at sharing a particular aspect of cooking around the rural art of pickling and water-bath canning. I will also share a word or two from my heart that has come out of my coffee time with God, who is good all the time. And all the time God is good. Incidentally, I've found out that our loving Lord is fond of pickles and preserves too, especially with His coffee.

Faith, Family & Community

I grew up in the rural community of Chandler, Texas. Chandler is ten or so miles due west of Tyler, Texas. Tyler is a city of approximately 100,000 in population. Chandler is a Neches River town that became a Lake Palestine (pronounced Pal-es-teén)

The Picklin' Parson's Cookbook

community when the river was dammed on the south gulf flowing end, in the late 1960s. When I was growing up, Chandler had a population of approximately 700; now it has a population near 3,000. My family's drugstore soda fountain was a community gathering spot when I was a kid. I dare say my father knew everyone in town. Churches were distinct and separate, but they came together for special events to accentuate "we have more in common than we have that separates us." It would have to be a very special occasion growing up to have involved the Black congregations in town, of which there were three. This value of coming together is such a need in our country today, and in the present church scene too.

What we knew—in the midst of rural life that even crossed racial divides—is that we ALL had in common the enjoyment of homemade food. Whether talking about family night fellowship dinners at the church, dinners on the grounds with other churches coming together, or at the kitchen tables in homes, so much of life was celebrated around good food. Saying "grace" around the tables said it all—the dinner, the fellowship, the food was a gift. And often you would hear—from the women usually—"This was delicious. I'd love to have that recipe." And long before there were church pictorial directories, there were church recipe books making the sharing of family food a community experience.

I do not remember life apart from church, and for me that was primarily at First United Methodist Church in Chandler, Texas. We shared revivals, Memorial Day dinners on the grounds and Vacation Bible School with other churches in town too. Church was the lifeblood of our community, and my family was there when the doors were open—every Sunday morning and Sunday night and the days in between. I had a sixteen-year Sunday School perfect attendance pin, which was no "big deal." Every other kid in church had one too. With no electronic diversions and with a good television antenna that enabled reception of three channels, the greatest entertainment and most substantial gatherings happened at church. It was not uncommon for me to be the fourth generation sitting on the pew, singing "Bringing in the Sheaves." Today, this would be understood as "quaint," but it was simply everyday life for me growing up.

At the age of fourteen, I knew God was calling me into ordained ministry as my lifelong profession. I preached my first sermon on the Sunday night after Christmas in 1975; I was sixteen years old. As I recall, the sermon went through Genesis to Revelation in ten minutes with my voice quivering and my knees knocking, but when I finished the greeting line was nothing short of a means of grace. You'd thought I was John Wesley himself the way the congregation made over me and encouraged me along my way.

The Picklin' Parson's Cookbook

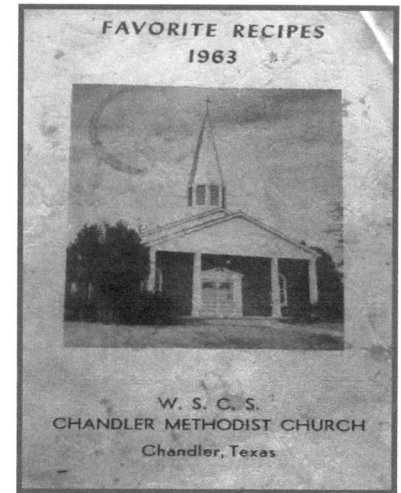

I count my upbringing as a blessing, my privilege in the best sense of the word, and a gift of grace and God's goodness. When I was born and into my childhood, I knew two of my great-great-grandmothers, three of my great-grandmothers, and two of my great-grandfathers. My paternal and maternal grandparents were very much a part of my childhood and young adulthood. Stories told about those grandparents that I didn't know are part of my consciousness of God's blessing. The extended family makes these characters come to life for me and informs my appreciation of family heritage and community connection. One example is the fall ribbon cane harvest and the cooking of syrup. One of the syrup operations featured President Montgomery. President, which was her name, was the matriarch of one of the black families in our town. She was the one called on to examine the consistency and taste of the syrup to say if it was ready or "good to go." Her grandson Spencer Montgomery Sr. told me this story that I recorded just months before his death. His great-grandmother Ella Higgins—"Aunt Eller" to my father and his friends in their childhood—will be featured later in a story. Nothing like ribbon cane syrup—the image of it covering a hot cast iron skillet of biscuits—to bridge the span of a racial divide.

Stories, Photos & Recipes

I shined shoes on Saturdays in Buford Ellis' barber shop next door to the drugstore; like my father had done before me. Buford would cut hair all day long with a King Edward cigar in his mouth, and most of the time it was lit. Nobody gave a hoot about secondhand smoke, though we should have. The old men who would loiter there, and the ones who were really there to get a haircut or a straight razor shave, were all caught up in the spinning of stories and the spilling of opinions—on politics, religion, farming, the weather, country ways and cooking. Conversation was ripe with gossip, prejudice, bigotry, laughter and profanity. Sometimes it wasn't fit for a child to overhear. But two dimes for a shine, in hopes of getting a quarter, was the purpose for my being there in the corner with my shine box.

Overhearing and then participating in the more wholesome conversations—whether in the barbershop, at family gatherings, in church, or at school—was a lesson in rural life and oral tradition that has fed my soul. It has also influenced me in my profession as a pastor, preacher, or "parson." Story is the thread that weaves this cookbook together and hopefully makes the source of the recipes come alive and be a blessing—touch from God—that brings joy, the second fruit of the Spirit. And my, my, my, how we need more blessings of joy amidst the complications and strife of life today.

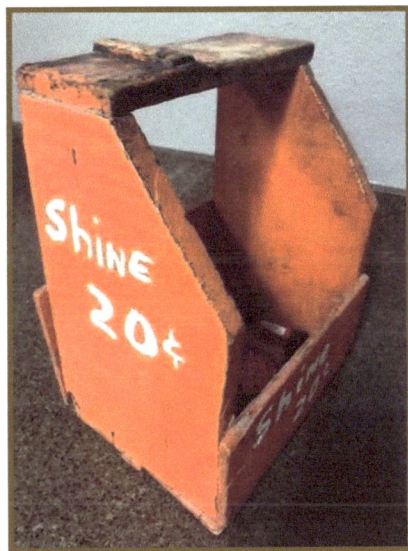

The Picklin' Parson's Cookbook

Photos are also a feature of the cookbook that are meant to bring focus to the stories and offer a view of jars of the finished products of the recipes. The old adage "a picture is worth a thousand words" is embraced. In part, the old photos are presented because the community of Chandler has virtually no old buildings remaining. A fire in the 1920s all but cleared out Main Street including my great-great-grandfather's and his twin brother's store, Ellis Brothers Grocery and Market store, though they built back. A tornado in the 1960s destroyed most of the upper levels of the old buildings on Broad Street—including my grandfather Copeland's, but he didn't build back. The remains of the buildings were demolished, making room for new development in the 1980s, which was focused on creating new space for the bank and convenience store, which now features a Texas staple—Whataburger.

All that is left of old Chandler is a few homes, the Chandler Museum & Visitor Center in former Sen. Ralph Yarborough's house, the old train depot, and photos. The photos shared in the cookbook will be presented primarily from my family's perspective but will also feature the broader history of Chandler. The photos have a personal meaning but are meant to largely celebrate family and community—whoever or wherever that might be for the reader. Several of the photos featured are on display in the Stillwater Farm Market Store & Dairy Shop on Main Street in Chandler. The photos are displayed there without explanation, unless I happen to be in the store to spin my version of the story behind the photo. The cookbook brings some of the story around the photos to print and enhances the retelling of the saga of what is Chandler. Other photos feature my family in the names—Ellis, Williams, Reagan (Mom's), Cade, Fitzgerald and Copeland (Dad's), as well as the African American families of Dewberry, Beasley, Frater, Montgomery, Higgins and Wallace.

The cookbook is being created in the year of Chandler's 140th anniversary as a way of saying "Happy Birthday" to a town that has marked me and will always be known to this "itinerant Methodist parson" as home. I resonate with the saying, "Home is where the heart is," and Chandler has a big part of my heart. I have also enjoyed rummaging through old church cookbooks and other family recipes written by hand, and pages loosely and carefully tucked into these cookbooks.

The oldest cookbook I have is *Favorite Recipes 1963 Women's Society of Christian Service Chandler Methodist Church*. The recipes were typed long before computers and printers. The cookbook came to be before the Methodist Church had united with the Evangelical United Brethren denomination and became the United Methodist Church. It was the product of the women of the church in an organization that became United Methodist Women—Women's Society of Christian Service or WSCS. I was four years old in 1963, and The Picklin' Parson's Cookbook my sister was born that year. No doubt, I was already enjoying the food cooked with the recipes in this book. I hope one day, five decades from now, people will value this book, half as much as I value this 1963 sacred relic.

Stillwater Farm—Generations in the Making

Stillwater Farm is the name I have given to my family's land that is a mile north, as the crow flies, of where once was the old community of "Stillwater." The farm is in the section of Fitzgerald farmland where my maternal grandmother—Alice Saphrona Fitzgerald Cade—was born in 1880, the same year that Chandler was founded. Benjamin and Josephine Saphrona Rise Fitzgerald were married in 1876, and in 1878, they purchased the farm two miles north of Chandler. They lived in a log barn on the property until their house could be built there. They had five sons and nine daughters. My great-grandmother Alice was the oldest daughter and third child born to the Fitzgeralds.

My grandmother—Rachel Cade Copeland, better known as "Gran"—wrote this history about her mother's family: "*The Fitzgeralds were living on their farm when Chandler was organized. Benjamin helped with the organization of the Chandler Methodist Church. Their membership was in Pleasant Retreat Methodist Church. There they attended camp meeting, reminding them of their Methodist days in North Carolina. Josephine prepared food to last the days of the revival. Benjamin was a successful farmer and rancher. He improved his place by planting fruit trees. Also grew ribbon cane and operated a syrup mill. Syrup was sold from this mill all over the area. There were fourteen children born to this union. They lost one child, Luster, at age six. Josephine died when she was forty years old. Benjamin reared the children that were still at home. Lena May, the youngest, was sixteen years of age when he died in 1916. I was eight years old when my grandfather Benjamin died. Many Saturdays he took me home with him on horseback. Sunday, we rode to church in the 'Surrey with the Fringe on Top.' He was a loving father and grandfather, a good neighbor and friend to all.*"

In 1901, Alice married Erasmus "Ras" Cade, the son of David and Mary Cade. These second-generation Chandlerites had four children: Mary Josephine (1902-1940), Luster Erasmus (1905-1946), Rachel (1908-1996), and Walter Connally (1911-1947). All of the children developed rheumatic fever in childhood that damaged their hearts. All the children but my grandmother Rachel died in their 30s and 40s. My great grandmother Alice was lovingly called "Nana." She was called this by many in town, but the ones who gave her that

name were her grandchildren: Jack Luster, Erasmus "Bud", Alice Murl, Vida Jo (my father's older sister), and my father — Don Cade Copeland — who was the youngest of the bunch.

Shortly after my great-great-grandpa Fitzgerald died, and the Fitzgerald section of land was acquired by Taylor and Jim to continue to farm, my great-grandfather Ras bought the adjoining property that is now the family farm. It was originally 60 acres of land contiguous to the Fitzgerald homeplace where Nana was born. It also adjoined the old Wiedman place that was near Farm to Market Road 2010. Daisy and Paul Young came to own the home that was built around the turn of the century, and the farm was very productive for crops and cattle. Gran and Daisy were good friends, and there was a berry patch on the far southeast part of the Young farm that adjoined my family's farm. Gran and Daisy loved to pick the blackberries and make jams, jellies and blackberry cobblers.

The east entrance of the farm features an old pear grove that was planted by Great-Grandpa Ras. Alice gave the land to her daughter—and only surviving child—Rachel. Rachel gave it to her son Don. Don and Martha Reagan Copeland—Mom and Dad—built on the homeplace in 2005. At that time, I made an offer on the Daisy and Paul Young property that adjoined the farm to the north. Mrs. Young sold us the acreage that now totals 30 acres and gives us an entrance to the farm from Farm to Market Road 2010, as well as the original entrance from County Road 3312.

The next year I was able to acquire the 30 acres to the north of the old farm place. The tracts combined now comprise 60 acres and adjoin the original farm which is approximately 65 acres. The farmland is rich, reddish, sandy loam—East Texas soil. In addition to the 100-year old pear trees, today Stillwater Farm features pecan, peach, and fig trees. Approximately 10 acres of irrigated row crop vegetables are also grown—Noonday sweet onions, garlic, watermelons, tomatoes, peas, squash, okra, peppers, sugar cane, etc.

The Market Store & Dairy Shop

The Stillwater Farm Market Store and Dairy Shop are in Chandler, Texas on W. Main Street, in a strip of shops in a commercial development called Old Main Street Station. Old Main Street was a thriving agrarian market area paralleling the railroad at the turn of the

The Picklin' Parson's Cookbook

20th century. The downtown featured two cotton gins, three packing sheds, a crating and canning factory and a plethora of businesses. Crops and produce were bought and sold, and commerce and community took place at the intersections of Broad Street (running north and south) and Main Street (running east and west). It was the downtown spot where much was happening.

In 2014, the Old Main Street Station started with Old Main Street Ice (phase 1) and Old Main Street Market Pavilion (phase 2). In the 1940s, Uncle Jim Fitzgerald built a barn out of the lumber of the old tomato sheds. The barn was to be torn down by its new owner in 2013, Mr. Randy Parker. I asked if I could have it for the lumber; he agreed, and the lumber was harvested and stored. Our son Zachary, who is an architect, designed the pavilion to showcase the lumber of the old tomato sheds. When the pavilion was constructed in 2015, the lumber was brought back to where it started 100 years ago. Old Main Street Shops (phase 3) opened in November of 2016 and Stillwater Farm Market Store and Dairy Shop was the first tenant.

The market store mimics the Ellis' old grocery and market stores, and the Stillwater Farm Market Store is a third-generation family grocery and market feature of our town. The Stillwater Farm Dairy Shop is a reminder of the old Copeland's Chandler drug store complete with a soda fountain. The Stillwater Farm Dairy Shop serves up lunches three days weekly, along with the best homemade ice cream in the area. The Market Floral Designs turns fresh flowers and plants into beautiful arrangements for occasions to bring joy and comfort.

A Mission, Values & Vision

The collective mission of our farm, store and shop is "Bringing carefully grown, farm-fresh goodness to kitchen tables everywhere." We seek to continue to grow a farm-to-market, market-to-table operation—serving a customer base with healthy, wholesome food products for personal and family enjoyment, along with beautiful gifts and floral designs for giving to family and friends. We value:

- Vibrant Communities—Chandler, Brownsboro, and Lake Palestine citizens are our home folks.
- Friendly Relationships—Customers and out-of-town guests are treated like "family."
- Carefully Grown Produce—Farm-raised produce from our farm and by trusted growers.
- Farm-Fresh Flowers—Floral arrangements and plants for personal enjoyment and sharing with others.

The Picklin' Parson's Cookbook

- Delightful Gifts—tins of pecans, jellies, salsas, cutting boards, soaps, etc.
- Homemade Food—"Homemade" best describes our daily lunches and sweet ice cream.

This cookbook comes to you right in the middle of a community and its history, a family and its stories, a store that features the produce that goes into the recipes and a shop that will feature this cookbook for your enjoyment. Enjoy the cookbook, for all that has gone into making it has been in hopes that God will use it to stir up more of the fruit of the Spirit in your life, in Chandler and other towns and cities, and in our nation and world.

> But what happens when we live God's way? He brings gifts into our lives, much the same way that fruit appears in an orchard—things like affection for others, exuberance about life, serenity. We develop a willingness to stick with things, a sense of compassion in the heart, and a conviction that a basic holiness permeates things and people. We find ourselves involved in loyal commitments, not needing to force our way in life, able to marshal and direct our energies wisely.
> Galatians 5:22

The Picklin' Parson's Cookbook

WATER-BATH CANNING
(A Good Pickle to be in)

&

BRINING and CRISPING

The Picklin' Parson's Cookbook

WATER-BATH CANNING

Equipment

Water bath canning is a simple process, and like most anything else, it becomes easier with practice. The equipment is essential, and most of it is part of every standard kitchen. There are, however, a few items that are large and necessary or are specific to the canning process. The investment in the proper equipment saves time and energy, helping to assure the cook that the jars of pickled vegetables, jellies, jams, preserves, and other homemade fruit delights will be handled and sealed properly.

- Large cooking pot
- Large canning pot
- Crock #3 or #5
- Large bowl
- Jar tongs
- Jar funnel
- Wooden stir spoons
- Knives
- Peeler
- Corer
- Strainer
- Ladle
- 8-cup measuring bowl
- Measuring spoons
- Mason jars, lids and bands

Sterilizing

"Clean and hot" is the goal set forth for all of the jars that will hold the canned products. Sterilizing can come from simply putting a clean jar in a large pot of boiling water, without the lids and bands. Also, keeping the jars hot until they are filled is a good practice. Hot filling in hot jars is the optimal way to can, and sterilizing is the next important step.

The Picklin' Parson's Cookbook

1. Preheat the oven to 225 degrees, and turn the oven off so it will remain a warm environment for the jars until time to can.
2. Sterilize jars, lids, and bands in boiling water for 2 minutes; then remove from the water with jar tongs.
3. Place jars on a cookie sheet with the open end up and place in the oven.
4. Place lids and bands on a clean towel to air dry then wipe dry with a paper towel.

Filling

After the cooking is done and the creation is ready to be placed in the jars for canning, all is ready for the step that requires a bit of careful handling. The most important utensils to have ready are the jar funnel and a ladle. Having a warm water wet paper towel to dry the rims is another important feature in filling the jars to keep the jar top and treads clean of the filling residue and dried of water to prevent rusting of the lid.

5. Remove jars from the oven and ready them for the funneling of the cooked mixture, fruit or vegetables.
6. Funnel the mixture into the jars—leaving ¾-inch headspace on quart, ½-inch on pint, and ¼-inch on cup jars.
7. Wipe the threads of the jars with a "hot-water wet" paper towel, and dry the threads with a paper towel to prevent rust.
8. Seal the jars with lids and hand tighten bands.

Sealing

When all of the jars are filled, and the large pot of water is boiling, all is ready for the final—and most important step—of sealing the jars. Remember to be careful in placing the jars in the water using the jar tongs. Keep the jars upright. Don't let them tip over and allow the jar filling to coat the upper part of the inside of the jar. The same care should be taken in removing the jars from the boiling water.

9. Place jars in a large canning pot of boiling water for 12 to 15 minutes with the jars fully immersed in the water.
10. Remove the jars with the jar tongs to a towel-lined counter or a rack.
11. Let cool to complete sealing. Listen for popping sound as the vacuum created by the cooling air in the jars seals them.

The Picklin' Parson's Cookbook

NOTE: A properly sealed jar can last in a cool closet out of direct sun for over a year. If any jars do not seal, store them chilled in the refrigerator. Opened jars should last one to two months in the refrigerator. Let sit 24 hours before eating.

BRINING & CRISPING

Fermenting Pickles

Pickling is the process of preserving food by anaerobic fermentation in brine or vinegar. The process my family used in pickling was brining and is a two-part process. The beginning was a style of fermenting, in essence, with basically soaking for one week in salt water. Though this process perhaps existed in my family for 10 generations, pickling began 4,000 years ago using cucumbers native to India and harvested in the Tigris Valley. The part of the process my family used was a seven-day process.

Although the process was invented to preserve foods, today, pickled foods are made and enjoyed because people like the way they taste. The term pickle is derived from the Dutch word "pekel," meaning brine or northern German "pökel," meaning salt or brine. Of course, brining was necessary before refrigeration to keep vegetables and meats preserved and safe for consumption. NOTE: Iodized salt in pickling is a no-no.

This wet-brining technique promotes the development of lactobacillus—a bacterium that works to break down sugars into lactic acid, a natural preservative. Over time, the vegetables will soften as if being gently cooked and take on a tangy, sour taste. The basic ratio my family and I used in the process is 3 cups of salt to 24 cups or 1 ½ gallons of water for any wet brine. If you're feeling fancy, throw in some smashed garlic cloves, peppercorns, and citrus (also smashed) or even a sweetener like honey, ribbon cane syrup, or brown sugar. The addition of "extras" infuses the vegetables and slightly flavors. The addition of the sweeteners also slightly browns the vegetables.

1. Add 1 c. of kosher salt or sea salt, or pickling salt, (NO iodized salt) to one gallon of water and bring it to a boil.
2. Pour over vegetables that are in a crock with a plate on top to make sure vegetables stay submerged.
3. Let stand in the brine for seven days. (It's a Godly creation.)
4. Every day skim the foam that rises to the surface of the brine.

The Picklin' Parson's Cookbook

I have added a feature of rinsing in ice cold water and letting the vegetables stand in the water for 1 hour, before returning them to the crock for the second or crisping stage that has already begun with the ice water bath.

Crisping Pickles

Alum is a chemical compound most commonly found in the form of potassium aluminum sulfate. Alum is added to pickles to create the classic crispness and crunch of a good dill pickle. According to the USDA, alum may still safely be used to firm fermented cucumbers, and it does not improve the firmness of quick-process pickles. The three-day process my family used definitely improves the crispness when followed as outlined.

1. On day 8, drain the brine in a place where vegetation will be impacted; do not pour down the sink.
2. Cut cucumbers into chunks (about ½ inch thick) or leave them whole, and place them in a bath of ice water for 1 hour.
3. Make a crisping solution with 2 tablespoons of alum to 1 ½ gallons of water in a large pot.
4. Bring the alum and water to a boil, and pour the crisping solution over the pickle chunks that are in the crock while the water is still boiling hot.
5. On day 9, (REPEAT) drain the crisping solution from the pickle chunks (no ice water bath required); make a new batch of crisping solution with water and alum and bring to a boil. Pour it over the pickles while it is still boiling hot.

The Picklin' Parson's Cookbook

PICKLED and SPICED

(And Everything Nice)

FRUIT & VEGGIES

The Picklin' Parson's Cookbook

A STORY
"Favit," "Yummy," "Boy in the Morning" & Family

It is fitting that the first picklin' recipe in this cookbook is one from Malisa Joanne Birdwell Ellis, known to most of her large family and many in the community of Chandler as Mawmaw Ellis. She was born on March 22, 1877, and she died on December 17, 1965. I was six years old when she died. She was born in Henderson County, Texas and so was her mother, Joanna Catherine Piles. She married my great-great-grandfather William Franklin "Mank" Ellis on May 27, 1894. My great-grandfather George Lafayette "Corbett" Ellis—who we called "Daddy Hacy"—was born within the first year of their marriage. Daddy Hacy was the oldest of their six children. Mamma Hacy (Laura Alice Williams Ellis) was married to my great-grandfather, and she was the one who helped take care of my sister Laura Jill and me. I learned much following her around the garden and the kitchen. More on that later.

The Ellis family headed for Texas from Alabama in October of 1870, in hopes of a better life post-Civil War. The trip in a covered wagon drawn by two oxen took 46 days and nights. There were no bridges to cross the rivers, creeks, and small streams. They ferried across the larger rivers and creeks. Finally, they made it to Van Zandt County, Texas, just outside of Edom to Uncle Alva Brewer's farm. Mank and his twin brother Mant were six-years-old when they made the trip.

The twins grew up together, farmed side-by-side, and were business partners, first building a cotton gin and a grist mill in Davidson, Texas. Then in 1912, they bought a grocery store in Chandler and relocated there. Clyde Ellis said in the book *Chandler: Its History and People*, "I remember 55 wooden barrels full of kraut from cabbage we had grown, drying peaches in the July and August sun on the wagon sheet placed on top of the cowshed; cooking hominy in a 30-gallon wash pot, later storing it in the crocks, churns and other earthen utensils."

Daddy Hacy and his first cousin Clyde bought the grocery store from their twin brother fathers in 1938 and continued to carry on the family business. I like to think that the Stillwater Farm Market Store is a third-generation family and Chandler business. I have a snapshot memory of Daddy Hacy, riding his beloved Palo, a big palomino horse. The cousins operated Ellis & Ellis Grocery until 1965 when Daddy Hacy—who had suffered a debilitating stroke—simply could not carry on the partnership.

The stroke paralyzed Daddy Hacy on his left side and left him unable to say much more than the phrase, "Boy, in the morning." With that clearly spoken phrase he communicated everything. He would get his point across by saying, "Boy, in the morning, boy in the morning, boy, boy, boy in the morning," while motioning with his good arm and pointing to what he wanted you to see. I loved my Daddy Hacy and can still feel his one-armed hugs at the side of his wheelchair, as he said, "Boy in the morning." I knew he was saying "Boy, I love you, and I'm proud of you." I could see it in his eyes.

I was six-years-old when Mawmaw Ellis died, and I vaguely remember her. My great-grandmother Mamma Hacy, on the other hand, was a grandparent that made quite an impression on me. My sister and I spent a lot of time with Mamma and Daddy Hacy growing up. Mamma Hacy was our babysitter during the day, while our mom taught school and our dad ran his pharmacy.

Mamma Hacy was a gardener par excellence. She grew a vegetable garden every year and also had pecan trees, pear trees, peach trees, fig trees and pomegranate bushes outside her kitchen window. I can see her now in her bonnet digging new potatoes with a tater fork, while humming all the time she gardened. For the most part, the gardening and farming bug that bit me did so long ago while walking with my bonnet-wearing Mamma Hacy.

Mamma Hacy was a "Williams," and the Williams sisters had a hometown reputation for their kitchen ways and techniques that made for excellent country cooking. One of the Williams sisters—Aunt Flora "Florie" Williams Dean—had a café (Dean's Café) in town during my growing up years. Incredible food and pies were served in her kitchen among other fried delights like chicken, steak, okra, squash, and green tomatoes. There was always an array of savory vegetables. Mamma Hacy was every bit the cook that her sister was, and she had a bright green thumb to boot. Mamma Hacy and Mawmaw Ellis were two strong women and two great cooks. They shared one another's recipes and honed one another's skills in the kitchen. There is no doubt that there was some innate cooking ability and that is a gift, but teaching others to cook to their own full potential was something they were glad to do. Along with skills and knowledge of the kitchen being passed down, so were recipes. They traveled with the people who moved from places like Virginia and the deeper South to East Texas. In these parts, they've been pickling and canning for decades. Mawmaw's Virginia Chunk Sweet Pickles recipe has been passed down to her descendants for many years.

The Picklin' Parson's Cookbook

I made the pickles this year and took great pride in knowing our first grandchild,—Claire Bear, an eighth generation Texan—was the seventh generation to enjoy Mawmaw's old-fashioned 12-day pickle recipe. When she tasted her first Mawmaw Ellis sweet pickles at the age of two-and-a-half, she said, "Ummmm, they my favit." Then I asked myself, "How could a Mawmaw Ellis who had rarely left the county and never left the state of Texas come up with a pickle recipe named after the state of Old Virginny?" A little ancestry work revealed that Mawmaw's great-grandparents were Robert and Jane Birdwell. They were both born in Virginia in 1751, twenty-five years before the Declaration of Independence. Could it be that this recipe was passed down from mothers to daughters, all the way from a Virginia origin? If so, our Claire Bear is the tenth-generation daughter to enjoy these Old Virginny treats, her "favit" sweet pickles.

I tried my hand at the second pickle recipe, which was Mamma Hacy's Bread and Butter Pickles. After a couple of tries, I think I have it. The onions, turmeric, garlic, and the spices—all making up that sweet, savory taste—are pure Mamma Hacy. The acid test, however, would be our two-and-half-year-old connoisseur Claire Bear. As she was at her tasting desk (high chair), donning her favorite bib, I wanted to see what she thought about my stab at Mamma Hacy's pickles. I put a few chunks on her plate, and she picked up her little fork with the animals on the handle. She forked a pickle, and put it in her mouth. As she chewed it, I waited for her honest critique. All of a sudden she shouted out, "Yummy! That's yummy!" A "yummy" is not really any better—nor is it any worse—than a "They my favit." I like to think that as I belted out a laugh at her response, her great-grandparents were laughing too from a heavenly perch. She's an Ellis alright and a Williams, so loving pickles is in her genes. "Boy in the morning!"

About the Recipes

The first two pickling recipes in this book feature the sweeter and savory version of cucumber delights. It's amazing that one can take a plain ol' cucumber and turn it into a chunk of taste bud-tingling goodness. The recipes are days in the making; therefore, pray for patience when making them. The pickler needs to relax into the process and anticipate each day, each step, bringing about a real creation. Enjoy yourself!

The Picklin' Parson's Cookbook

1
MAWMAW'S VIRGINIA CHUNK
SWEET PICKLES (A Twelve-Day Process)

Ingredients

- 100 cucumbers
- 1 ½ gallons of water
- 3 c. of pickling salt
- 12 c. cider vinegar
- ¾ c. kosher salt
- 32 red chile de árbol peppers (little dried peppers)
- 8 c. of sugar
- ½ c. mustard seeds
- ¼ c. cloves, ground
- ¼ c. coriander seeds
- ¼ c. red pepper flakes
- ¼ c. fennel seeds
- ¼ c. celery seeds
- ¼ c. black or mixed peppercorns
- 3 Gallons of water
- 4 Tbsp. Alum

Readying

On day 1, cut about ¼ off the blossom end of the cucumber, and place the whole cucumbers in a crock. Make a brine of a proportion of 3 cups salt (pickling salt) to 1 ½ gallons of water in a large pot and bring to a boil. Pour the brine (salt water) over the cucumbers that are in the crock while it is still boiling hot. Let stand for 7 days, skimming daily the foam that rises to the surface.

Note: Always brine at room temperature.

The Picklin' Parson's Cookbook

Crisping

On day 8, safely discard the brine. Cut the cucumbers into pickle chunks about ½ inch thick and place them in a bath of ice water; let stand for 1 hour. Make a crisping solution with 2 Tbsp. of alum to 1 ½ gallons of water in a large pot. Bring the alum and water to a boil, and pour the boiling crisping solution over the pickle chunks that are in the crock. On day 9, drain the crisping solution from the pickle chunks. Make a new batch of crisping solution with water and alum and bring to a boil. Pour it over the pickles while it is still boiling hot.

Spicing

On day 10, drain the crisping solution from the pickle chunks, and leave them in the crock. Place the vinegar 5 cups of sugar, salt, and spices in a pot and bring to a boil. Pour over the pickles that are in the crock while the spice mixture is still boiling hot. On day 11, strain the pickles from the spicy syrup, retaining the spicy syrup; bring the spice mixture to a boil adding 2 cups of sugar. Leave the pickle chunks in the crock. Again, pour over the pickles.

Filling & Canning

On day 12, preheat the oven to 225 degrees, and place the canning jars right-side up on a baking sheet. Place them in the oven to keep them hot. Repeat the process of the prior day, but add only 1 cup of sugar. Pour the mixture over the pickles that are in the crock while it is still boiling hot. Ladle and funnel the pickles and syrup into each jar. Position a couple of dried pepper pods in each pint jar. Double the amounts for a quart jar. Make sure all air bubbles are out of the jar, and the liquid completely covers the pickles just below the ½ inch of headspace. Follow a standard water bath practice for canning and sealing by submerging each filled jar into the boiling water with jar tongs to boil on a low boil for 15 minutes. The process should yield 16 pints or 8 quarts.

The Picklin' Parson's Cookbook

2
CREATION BREAD & BUTTER PICKLES
(A Seven-Day Process)

Ingredients

- 12 lbs. of cucumbers (approximately 1 peck)
- 4 onions, sweet and smaller
- 4 onions, purple and smaller
- 2 c. salt
- 4 Tbsp. alum
- Water
- 1 gallon white vinegar
- 3 c. sugar
- 1/2 c. pickling spice
- 1 Tbsp. turmeric
- 1 Tbsp. mustard seeds
- 1 tsp. celery seeds
- ½ tsp. cloves, ground
- 6 or 8 turmeric roots, in thin decorative slices

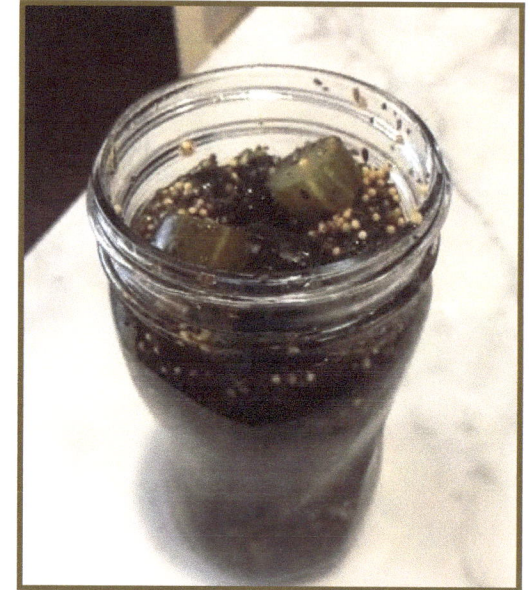

Readying

Day One—Soak the cucumbers in ice cold water for 30 minutes. Drain them and trim off the blossom ends of the cucumbers. Slice them into 1/2″ slices, or slightly larger chunks. Pack the pickle pieces into a crock or a large pickle jar. Add two cups of pickling salt to one gallon of water. Bring the mixture to a rolling boil, and pour it over the pickles. Cover the container, and let it sit overnight.

Crisping

Day Two and Day Three—Drain the salt water mixture off the pickles. Add 2 Tbsp. of alum to one gallon of water, and bring it to a rolling boil. Pour the alum water over the pickles. Cover and let it sit at room temperature overnight.

The Picklin' Parson's Cookbook

Cooking

Day Four—Drain the alum water off the pickles and dispose of it. Bring the white vinegar with the 4 cups of sugar and the spices to a rolling boil. Pour the spicy cider syrup over the pickles. Cover, and let it sit overnight. Day Five—Drain the spicy cider syrup off of the pickles, and retain it in a pot. Add one more cup of sugar, and bring the spicy cider syrup to a rolling boil. Pour the spicy syrup over the pickles. Cover, and let it sit overnight. Day Six—Drain the spicy cider syrup off of the pickles, and retain it in a pot. Carefully slice the onions into disks with a mandolin slicer, and add them to the pickles. Only if you want the pickles sweeter, add one more cup of sugar. Bring the spicy syrup to a rolling boil. Pour the spicy syrup over the pickles and onions. Cover, and let it sit overnight.

Filling & Canning

Day Seven—Preheat the oven to 225 degrees and place the pint jars right-side up on a baking sheet. Place them in the oven to keep them hot. Drain the spicy cider syrup off of the pickles and onions, and retain it in a pot. Bring the spicy cider syrup to a rolling boil. Transfer the pickles and onions from the crock to a large bowl. Pour the boiling spicy syrup over the pickles and onions. Ladle and funnel the pickles and syrup into each jar. Position a couple of turmeric slices in each pint jar. Double the amounts for a quart jar. Make sure that all air bubbles are out of the jar, and the liquid completely covers the pickles just below the ½ inch of headspace. Follow a standard water bath practice for canning and sealing by submerging each filled jar into the boiling water with jar tongs to boil on a low boil for 15 minutes. The process should yield 10 pints or 5 quarts.

The Picklin' Parson's Cookbook

A STORY
A Handful of Pickle, A Heart Full of Coach & Pickles

Pickles always remind me of little league baseball. My summers growing up were spent on my bike as my means of travel and in large part at the baseball field. The ballfield was behind the Chandler Elementary School that was built after the Depression by the Works Project Administration (WPA). The school building featured the large iron ore rocks of our area that also comprised the rock wall that completely surrounded the campus, including the ballfield. Behind the backstop fence and toward the westside back wall was a feature that added so much to the ballgame atmosphere, truly making the games events. It was the concession stand.

The concession stand was a little shack of sorts, barely big enough for one worker to navigate from the snow cone machine to the candy display. And there on the counter, amidst the candy concessions was a tall jar full of big, juicy dill pickles. They sat there in the sour juice as a delightful contrast to the sweet, syrupy, ice cold snow cones and the bars of candy meant to satisfy any sweet tooth. If one has a sweet tooth, then how many teeth in one's head long for the taste of a sour, dill pickle? Sometimes you just have to have a treat so tart that it will make you display a crinkled face with every sour bite. I loved to get a big pickle, which was a handful, all wrapped in paper. The big dills on a hot summer night, were the perfect face-crinkling treat to accompany watching the older pony league boys play ball. It all made for a pickle-eating good time, allowing for better grips on the bats and a sticky-handlebars bike ride home.

Our little league coach was Mr. John Nash, who was the Union Boss at the Kelly Springfield Tire plant five miles from Chandler toward Tyler on Highway 31. Mr. Nash was not so tall but oh so stout. He had a neat cut flattop, a barrel chest and looked like he could take out any Marine sergeant. He had a gentle side with us kids, a patient demeanor, and the kindest, bluest eyes. Many men in Chandler were employed at the huge tire plant to build tires for shipments all over the country. They were part of the labor union, and Mr. Nash was their representative, spokesman and negotiator. His job was to keep things right and fair for the workers. Coach Nash had a 1956 model Ford pickup that was a light green color with its rounded, sturdy look. Back in the day, this is the way we would travel to out-of-town games as the ragtag Chandler Tigers little league team, donning the red and white. There was room for two of the older boys in the cab of

The Picklin' Parson's Cookbook

the truck with the coach. The rest of us would pile in the bed of the truck—unseatbelted of course—with our bat bag thrown in on top. This was our open-air-conditioned ride to whatever little town we were to play in.

I really didn't notice in the late 1960s as a not-yet teenager, but our team was different from the other teams we played in the little towns like Brownsboro, Murchison, Edom, Ben Wheeler, and the unincorporated community of Bethel. The red and white Chandler Tigers were made up of black and white kids. Our black school classmates, Marvin, Jake and Poochie Montgomery; Dexter Simpson; and Buck Hendrix were part of our school and part of our team. We didn't know it then—but came to know in later years—some teams wouldn't play the Tigers just because of who we were; you might say our stripes were different. Coach Nash, on the other hand, treated us all the same. He never exposed us to the ugliness that some coaches and fans were having to work through and get over.

It is said that Chandler was the first town in the state of Texas to desegregate its school. I never knew a school experience in Chandler that was segregated. I started first grade at Chandler Elementary School in the fall of 1965 with Spencer Montgomery, Dexter Simpson, Vickey Beasley and Donna Smith, along with the rest of us dozen white children. We had lost our high school the year prior, which is a sad story indeed involving race and politics.

Integration started earlier in our area than in some East Texas towns that had wealthier districts and were more homogenous in population. The choice to integrate was unpopular with some. The decision to integrate was driven by the fact that Chandler's school district was small with an inadequate tax base. The school was below the student-to-teacher ratio required by the state. The school district simply didn't have enough money and didn't have enough students. Also, the nation's desegregation legislation that was dreamed of by Dr. Martin Luther King Jr. and initiated by President John Fitzgerald Kennedy was championed by Texan and President of the United States of America Lyndon Baines Johnson. The legislation was partly authored by Chandler's heralded son, U.S. Sen. Ralph Webster Yarborough, who was a brilliant lawyer. In 1964, it was all but passed by Congress.

The decision was made to close the black school in Chandler and join the students with Chandler Elementary and High School. The closing of the black school and integrating the white school would produce the student-to-teacher ratio that was required. A few upset families chose to buy a bus and transport their children to Van High School, some 17 miles away. This, of course, was to avoid the

The Picklin' Parson's Cookbook

desegregation of Chandler schools, but no one could bus beyond the civil rights legislation that was fast becoming law. The loss of students put Chandler's schools out of compliance with the state law related to student-teacher ratio. This reality, along with the small tax base of the school district, resulted in Chandler's school system going broke—belly up, which also led to the end of the proud red and white Tigers. This uproar was over the ugly matter of separation, and this parson says our sin surrounding black and white children of God and where they would go to school and participate in school activities, including athletics. This matter will be addressed later in this book regarding our history. We all knew when we lost our school that we were destined to become proud Brownsboro Bears and don the blue and gold. Our rivals would become our family. We little leaguers were holding on to the last bastion of being Tigers. We stood tall wearing red and white uniforms with Texas Pecan Nursery (our sponsor) on our jersey backs above our numbers. Amidst the unrest and ugliness rose champions of justice and equality who did the hard, caring and complicated work regarding race relations. One example came about in 1980, in the year when Chandler was celebrating its Centennial and the City Council had an opening. Mayor Kenneth Cade appointed Mr. John Milton Wallace, a member of a longstanding family of citizens of the town, and one who was highly respected, to be the first Black representative on the City Council.

My heart goes out to one of those unsung champions, our Coach Nash. I remember once that Coach Nash got into a scuffle with another coach. It wasn't over an umpire's call; it was over something that was said about one of our Tigers. We were a team, and Coach Nash was the tough, caring, representative champion that we needed, just as did the tire workers. Some things for him were beyond negotiation and simply talking about. It was time to accept needed change and move forward, and the coach was the man to "crank the old truck" and get it moving. Coach Nash was a great coach, but he was—and is—a better man. He was especially good at such a time for us little leaguers, U.S. citizens accustomed to rural life that had to change for the better of all. We looked up to Coach Nash and knew that he always had our backs. He knew we were just kids who loved playing baseball, and most of us loved big dill pickles. But all of us deserved a chance to play ball together.

"You're blessed when you've worked up a good appetite for God.
He's food and drink in the best meal you'll ever eat.
You're blessed when you care. At the moment of being "care-full," you find yourselves cared for.
You're blessed when you get your inside world—your mind and heart—put right. Then you can see God in the outside world.
You're blessed when you can show people how to cooperate instead of compete or fight.
That's when you discover who you really are, and your place in God's family.
Matthew 5:6-9

About the Recipes
There are two dill pickle recipes for you to enjoy whether it brings back little league memories or not. You can enjoy them around the kitchen table or if you're in Chandler, go to the new elementary school and stand close to a part of the old rock wall, open a jar, and eat a pickle. If you listen closely, you can hear the sounds of days gone by; the ump calls, "Strike one!" And a little kid says, "One big dill pickle, please."

The Picklin' Parson's Cookbook

3
LITTLE LEAGUE BIG DILL PICKLES

Ingredients

- 100 cucumbers (As big as you want them)
- 1 ½ gallons of water
- 3 cups of pickling salt
- 2 Tbsp. dried dill seed
- 24 garlic cloves
- 2 large sweet onions, peeled and quartered
- 7 grape leaves or oak leaves
- 3 Tbsp. of alum
- 4 c. apple cider vinegar
- ¾ c. kosher salt
- ½ c. mustard seeds
- ¼ c. coriander seeds
- 24 red chile de árbol peppers
- 12 fresh dill heads

Readying

On day 1, cut about ¼ off of the blossom end of the cucumbers, and place the whole cucumbers in a crock. Make a brine of a proportion of 3 cups salt (pickling salt) to 1 ½ gallons of water in a large pot and bring to a boil. Pour the brine (salt water) over the cucumbers that are in the crock while it is still boiling hot. Let stand for 7 days, skimming daily the foam that rises to the surface.

Crisping

On day 8, safely discard the brine. Place the whole pickles in a bath of ice water, and let stand for 1 hour. Make a crisping solution with 2 Tbsp. of alum to 1 ½ gallons of water in a large pot. Bring the alum and water to a boil, and pour the boiling crisping solution over the pickle chunks that are in the crock. On day 9, drain the crisping solution from the pickles. Put the pickles back in the crock with 7

The Picklin' Parson's Cookbook

grape leaves. Make a new batch of crisping solution with 1 Tbsp. of alum and 1 ½ gallons of water and again bring it to a boil. Pour it over the pickles and the grape leaves.

Cooking

On day 10, drain the crisping solution from the pickles, and leave them in the crock. Place the vinegar, salt, garlic, árbol chile peppers, seeds and dill heads in a pot and bring to boil. Pour over the pickles that are in the crock while the spice mixture is still boiling hot.

Filling & Canning

Preheat the oven to 225 degrees, and place the canning jars right-side up on a baking sheet. Place them in the oven to keep them hot. Place half of the pickles in the jars, filling the jars half full with the pickles (retaining the remaining pickles). Fill the jars half full with the hot liquid, and place 2 cloves of garlic, an árbol pepper pod, and dill head in each pint jar. Double the amounts for a quart jar. Put a few more pickles in the jars, and fill the jars with the hot liquid leaving ½ inch of headspace. Make sure all air bubbles are out of the jars. Follow a standard water bath practice for canning by submerging each filled jar into the boiling water with jar tongs to boil on a low boil for 15 minutes. The process should yield 12 pints or 6 quarts.

4
KITCHEN TABLE PICKLES

Ingredients

- 12 lbs. cucumbers
- 3 gallons water
- 3 c. pickling salt
- 2 Tbsp. dried dill seed
- 24 garlic cloves
- 5 large sweet onions, peeled and sliced into rings ¼-inch thick
- 7 grape leaves or oak leaves
- 3 Tbsp. of alum
- 4 c. apple cider vinegar
- ¾ c. kosher salt
- ½ c. mustard seeds
- ¼ c. coriander seeds
- 12 fresh dill heads
- 12 baby carrots

NOTE—Place the cucumbers in the crock and in a separate large cooking pot; then boil the water and ingredients. Do not boil the leaves, or the alum can be used at this time.

Readying

On day 1, cut about ¼ off of the blossom end of the cucumbers, and place the whole cucumbers in a crock. Make a brine of a proportion of 3 cups pickling salt to 1 ½ gallons of water in a large pot, and bring to a boil. Pour the brine (salt water) over the cucumbers that are in the crock while it is still boiling hot. Let stand for 7 days, skimming daily the foam that rises to the surface.

Crisping

On day 8, safely discard the brine. Place the whole pickles in a bath of ice water, and let stand for 1 hour. Make a crisping solution with 2 Tbsp. of alum to 1 ½ gallons of water in a large pot. Bring the alum and water to a boil, and pour the boiling crisping solution over the pickles that are in the crock. On day 9, drain the crisping solution from the pickles. Put the pickles back in the crock with 7 grape leaves. Make a new batch of crisping solution with 1 Tbsp. of alum and 1 ½ gallons of water, and again bring it to a boil. Pour it over the pickles and the grape leaves. Note: See the Brining & Crisping method described on page 41.

Cooking

On day 10, rinse the pickles and place in ice cold water for 30 minutes. Preheat the oven to 225 degrees, and place the canning jars right-side up on a baking sheet. Place them in the oven to keep them hot. Place half of the pickles in the jars, filling the jars half full with the pickles (retaining the remaining pickles). Place the vinegar, salt, garlic, carrots, seeds and dill heads in a cooking pot and bring to boil.

Filling & Canning

Place pickles in the jars half full with the pickles (retaining the remaining pickles). Fill the jars half full with the hot liquid and place 2 cloves of garlic, a pepper pod, several carrot slices, a few onion rings, and a dill head in each pint jar. Put the remaining pickles in the jars and fill the jars with the hot liquid leaving ½ inch of headspace. Make sure all air bubbles are out of the jar, and the liquid completely covers the pickles that are just below the headspace. Follow a standard water bath practice for canning and sealing by submerging each filled jar into the boiling water with the jar tongs to boil on a low boil for 15 minutes. The process yields 12 pints or 6 quarts.

A STORY
Limpin' Susan, Hoppin' John, Aunt Eller & Okry

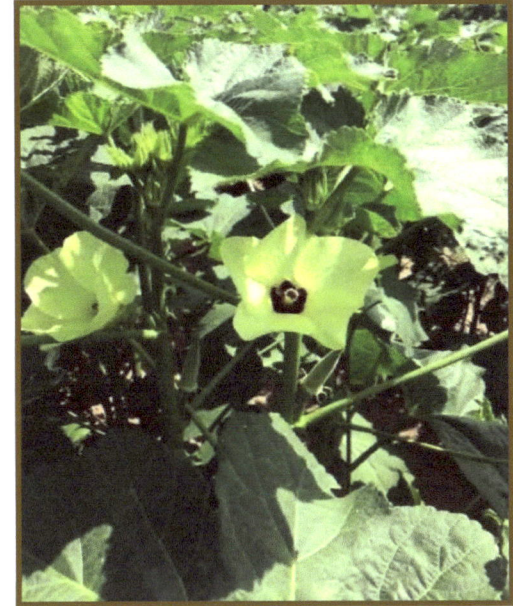

If you ever talk to an East Texas old timer, you may hear the word spelled o-k-r-a pronounced "okry." I don't really know why. It's an East Texan thing, but sometimes we East Texans can be a little different. Okry is a little different too, as far as veggies go. If you have ever planted okry, you know what I'm talking about; you don't let this pretty, little, yellow hibiscus-looking flower fool you. There is little that is nice about an okra plant. You plant okry a little later in the season because it likes warm soil;the hotter the weather, the more it seems to like life, and that's a little different. And once okry starts makin', it is relentless.

Relentless because it is at its best when it is small—3" to 4" and tender. Therefore, picking has to be regular, and if you have more than a few rows, daily pickin' is required. Okry also grows among its sticky, itchy, wear-you-out leaves. A pass or two of pickin' in the okry patch in a short sleeve shirt will give you a full-day of relentless regret. Yet, it's worth dealing with "relentless" just to taste this veggie. And I love it in its pure slimy form mixed with tomatoes, fried up in gold brown pieces, a staple part of a gumbo, baked or grilled with olive oil. Best of all, you can eat orky pickled with garlic or turmeric root as a snappy, savory morsel that it's hard for anyone not to enjoy.

How did this veggie make its way to the United States? Here's a little history brought to us by Michael W. Twitty (No kin to Conway). He said, "*Okra is an ancient vegetable that originated in southern Ethiopia thousands of years ago. It provides thickness and savor in the one-pot stews that are the basis of many traditional African diets. Spreading across the continent of Africa, it eventually came to be known by the tribal people of Western Africa and has been a staple in African and African diaspora cuisine for a long time. From the Igbo language of southeastern Nigeria, we get the vegetable's English name, as 'okwuru' became 'ochra' and 'okra'* (and in East Texas, 'okry').

In mainland North America, okra was one of the ultimate symbols of the establishment of the enslaved community as a culinary outpost of West Africa. Our best guess is that it came here at the start of the 18th century. Charleston and New Orleans were early hotbeds of okra cookery for certain, but okra was not confined to the Caribbean outposts of the Old South. Peter Kalm discussed okra in his American travels as a popular plant for soups among blacks and whites in the 1740's. Thomas Jefferson lauded it as one of Virginia's esteemed garden

The Picklin' Parson's Cookbook

plants in the 1780s, and references to okra can be found in garden records and maps across the early Mid-Atlantic, Chesapeake and Lower South.

For enslaved cooks, okra was a common thread in their mixed African heritage. Okra was most often prepared in a peppery stew that was eaten with rice, millet, hominy or corn mush. It was boiled with onions and tomatoes in a saucy preparation that was eaten in the same manner, or it was boiled on its own as a fresh vegetable. Okra with rice was called 'Limpin' Susan,' the cousin dish to cowpeas and rice, or 'Hoppin' John.' It was also boiled up with cowpeas for another dish, fried in small pieces with the boiled leaves served as a leafy green."

Who knows, but maybe one of Chandler's best cooks brought okry to us over 100 years ago. Jim Sidney Powell tells a story in *Way Back When*, about one who just might have been the very one. He writes, "*We Chandler residents knew her as Aunt Eller. Her house was located on the branch just south of the railroad tracks and just west of the Ellis Truck Parking lot. She was born sometime before the beginning of the Civil War in 1861, and she and her family were slaves. Spencer Montgomery, her great grandson and a local Chandler resident, said, 'I can remember my great-grandmother telling me on several occasions that she was a young girl during the Civil War.' The accompanying photo of Aunt Eller was taken in 1926 and hangs in the Stillwater Farm Market Store. She died twenty-three years after that picture was taken, it was 1949.' And she is said to have been over 100 years old.*

Aunt Eller was a hard-working independent woman who raised a family and cooked for Chandler's Joe Cade family, consisting of Mr. and Mrs. Cade and at one time seven of the Cade children. She worked for the Cade family well into her 70s. Aunt Eller, a superb cook, never used a recipe. She would combine the right proportions of the ingredients from her memory and produce taste-tempting dishes. Spencer said he could remember Aunt Eller crumbling leftover cornbread, adding ingredients to it, and serving it to their family. If a family member asked, 'What is this?' she replied, 'Just eat it and hush.'

The Picklin' Parson's Cookbook

Many times, she could be seen sitting on her front porch facing the railroad track, gently fanning with a funeral home fan or shelling a bushel of peas. All the while she'd be telling her grandkids and great grandkids stories about her life when she was growing up and how to be kind and polite to people. Aunt Eller would welcome me when I came to her house and played and went crawfishing in Aunt Eller's Branch with her great-grandsons, Percy Burns and his brother Mason."

About the Recipes

Relentless though okra may be, it is delicious in so many different forms. I will be offering two recipes, Pickled Garlic Okry and Trinity Savory Okra, that I have put together on my own. Leave it up to a parson to label a recipe "Trinity" that takes three days to make, but it is heavenly, if I say so myself. The Garlic Pickled Okry won a blue ribbon at the State of Texas Fair 2020. Okra is the sort of veggie that lends itself to the imagination and bit of creative license. In other words, "It's pretty hard to mess it up." Enjoy and thanks Aunt Eller for inspiring all that one could do with an okry pod.

5
PICKLED GARLIC OKRY

Ingredients

- 8 lbs. fresh okra (3 to 4 inches long)
- 16 large garlic cloves, peeled
- 16 ¼"-thick slices of lemon
- 6 c. of cider vinegar
- 4 c. of water
- ¾ c. kosher salt
- ½ c. sugar
- ½ c. of mustard seeds
- ¼ c. of coriander seeds
- ¼ c. red pepper flakes
- ¼ c. fennel seeds
- ¼ c. celery seeds
- ¼ c. black or mixed peppercorns

Readying

Preheat the oven to 225 degrees and place sterilized pint jars right-side up on a baking sheet. Place them in the oven to keep them hot. Wash the fresh okra pods thoroughly and trim the stem ends to 1/4-inch while being careful not to cut into the larger pod, leaving a nub of stem. Boil a large pot of water and blanch the okra in the boiling water for two minutes, removing the pods with the strainer and setting them aside. Put all pickling spices in a small bowl, and stir them to combine all of the spices. Thinly slice the lemons and set aside.

Cooking

Place the vinegar, water, salt, sugar and spices in a cook pot, and bring to a boil to dissolve the salt and sugar. Reduce heat and keep hot.

The Picklin' Parson's Cookbook

Filling & Canning

Remove the jars from the oven and place them on the baking sheet on the counter. Add a tablespoon of the mixed pickling spices to each pint jar. Double the amounts for a quart jar. With a plastic gloved hand arrange the okra in each jar with the first layer stem down and point end up. Position the one or two garlic cloves in each jar so that they can be seen with the okra. Push the remaining pods point end down between the pods, making an attractive presentation in the jar. Fill the pint or quart jars with the hot liquid, leaving ½ inch headspace. Make sure all air bubbles are out of the jar, and the liquid completely covers the pods that are just below the headspace. Follow a standard water bath practice for canning and sealing by submerging each filled jar into the boiling water with jar tongs to boil on a low boil for 15 minutes. The process should yield 10 pints or 5 quarts.

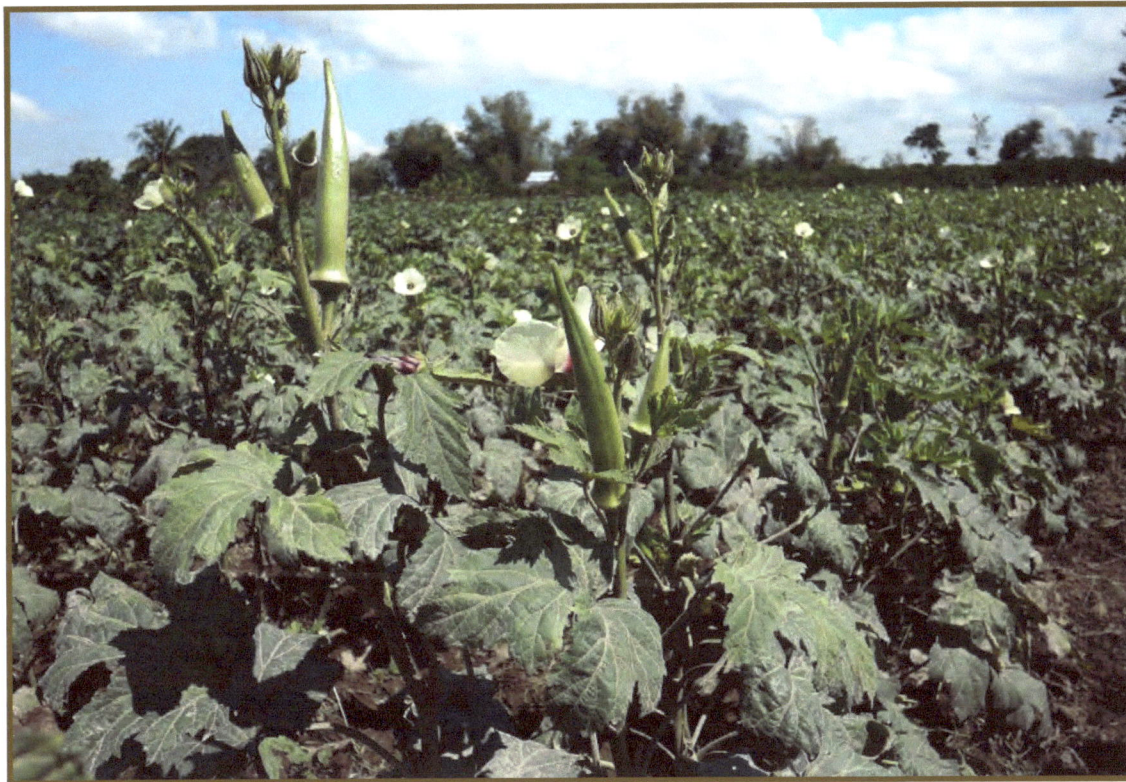

The Picklin' Parson's Cookbook

6
TRINITY SAVORY OKRA

Ingredients

- 8 lbs. fresh okra (3 to 4 inches long)
- 10 large garlic cloves, peeled
- 16 ¼"-thick slices lemon (approximately 4 lemons)
- 4 medium onions, sliced into rings
- 2 c. pickling salt
- 2 Tbsp. alum
- 3 gallons water
- 6 c. apple cider vinegar
- 4 c. water
- 3 c. kosher salt
- 3 c. sugar
- 1/2 c. pickling spice
- 1 Tbsp. turmeric
- 1 Tbsp. mustard seeds
- 1 tsp. celery seeds
- ½ tsp. cloves, ground
- Turmeric roots cut into slivers
- 20 dried red chile de árbol peppers

Readying

On day 1, wash the okra and trim the stems of the pods, not cutting down to the larger part of the pod. Soak it in ice cold water for 30 minutes; then, drain it from the water. Bring a pot of water to a boil, and blanch the okra pods for 1 to 2 minutes, removing them from the boiling water to a crock or a huge jar (not metal). Carefully slice the onions into thin rings with a mandolin slicer, and add them to the okra. Add two cups of pickling salt to 1/1/2 gallons water. Bring the mixture to a rolling boil. Let it cool, and pour it over the okra, covering all of the pods. Cover the container, and refrigerate overnight.

The Picklin' Parson's Cookbook

Crisping

On day 2, drain the salt water mixture off the pods and onions, and discard responsibly. Add 2 Tbsp of alum to 1 ½ gallons water, and bring it to a rolling boil. Let the mixture cool, and pour the alum water over the okra and onions. Cover the container, and refrigerate overnight.

Cooking

On day 3, drain the alum water off of the okra and onions, and dispose of it responsibly. Rinse the okra and onions, and set aside in the crock. Bring the apple cider vinegar, 2 sugar, and spices to a rolling boil. Let the syrup cool, and pour the spicy syrup over the okra and onions. Cover and let it sit for 6 to 8 hours. Preheat the oven to 225 degrees, and place the sterilized pint jars right-side up on a baking sheet. Place them in the oven to keep them hot. Drain the spicy syrup off of the okra and onions, and retain it in a pot, while setting the okra and onions aside in a bowl. Add one more cup of sugar and bring the spicy syrup to a rolling boil.

Filling & Canning

On day 3 1/2, remove the pint jars from the oven on the baking sheet, and place on the counter. Transfer the okra and onions to the hot jars, and fill them half full of okra neatly in a row with the pointy end up. Pour the spicy syrup over the okra and onions to about half-jar full. Add a sliver of turmeric root, a couple of dried red chile árbol peppers, and a garlic clove, so they can be clearly seen in the pint jar. Double the amounts for a quart jar. Finish packing the okra pods with points down, and top off the jar with the syrup, leaving ½-inch headspace in each pint jar. Make sure all air bubbles are out of the jar, and the liquid completely covers the pods that are just below the headspace. Follow a standard water bath practice for canning and sealing by submerging each filled jar into the boiling water with jar tongs to boil on a low boil for 15 minutes. The process should yield 10 pints or 5 quarts.

The Picklin' Parson's Cookbook

A STORY
Chandler's Version of the Mamas and the Papas & 'Maters

My hometown of Chandler, Texas, once had two cotton gins, three tomato packing sheds (one was sometimes called a peach packing shed), a crate factory and a peach canning factory. In the tomato sheds for several weeks in the summer, the women graded and sorted the tomatoes and put them into crates. The men stacked and loaded the crates onto the railcars on the tracks next to the sheds. And the kids? They played their hearts out in the wooden sheds and space just outside the open-air structures. Tomatoes and peaches were the main crops to be packed and shipped, but other produce—sweet onions, potatoes, pears etc.—would also be graded, sorted and shipped west from the sheds.

The local farmers could grow their crops in larger quantities with the assurance of a place to go with them once they were ready. Here is how the process worked according to Jim Sidney Powell as recorded in his book *Way Back When*: *"Area farmers—who started picking green tomatoes at sunrise—loaded them onto their sideboard trucks in bushel baskets and hauled them to the tomato sheds. Tomato buyers were on hand to purchase the tomatoes from the farmers. Good tomatoes would sell for around a dollar or two dollars per bushel. Dozens of loaded pickups or trucks lined up to be unloaded at the tomato sheds.*

After the tomatoes were unloaded, they were weighed. Then they were dumped onto the grader, a large piece of machinery that contained rotating wooden rollers on which the tomatoes traveled. Tomato graders lined up on each side [of the shed] separated the "culls" from the good tomatoes. The culls and empty baskets were weighed. That weight was deducted from the original weight, and the farmer was paid for only the good tomatoes.

The next step in the tomato shipping process showed my mother's talent and expertise as a tomato packer. Mama and her "packer" friends stood in a line behind packing stands next to bins of tomatoes. Each stand held a wooden box called a lug. The lugs were constructed on-site and came down an overhead chute to the packing stands. Mother would pick up a tomato from the bin in her left hand and—at the same time—pick up a square piece of thin, waxy tissue paper with her right hand. In one quick motion, she would slap the tomato into the

The Picklin' Parson's Cookbook

Chandler's "Tomato Packin' Mamas"

paper and loosely wrap it. She placed the wrapped tomatoes, double decked, in rows in the lug. A friendly competition existed among the packers who were usually all women. Each packer was paid a certain amount for each lug she packed.

When the lug was full, Mama would lift it and set it on a line of metal rollers. At this point, she marked the lug with her assigned number using a waxed crayon. The rollers carried the lugs to the topper machine where a "lug topper" pressed a slatted wooden lid down on top of the lug, so that he could secure it with nails. Around 700 lugs were then loaded on each refrigerated railroad car. The refrigeration came from large blocks of ice that were dropped down into bins on each end of the railcar. The tomato-laden boxcars were picked up each day and taken by freight train to their final destination west of here.

Tomato packin' was very physical and tiring to Mama because she had to stand on her feet all day and lift the heavy lugs onto the rollers. It was not uncommon for her to work from mid-morning to late at night. Although we hate that she had to work so hard and such long hours, our family needed the extra income.

The Stillwater Farm Market Store and all of the shops of the Old Main Street Station are in the very place where the tomatoes were once packed and shipped to destinations west. In the store, we post these old photos of the packers and what we've dubbed "Chandler's Tomato Packing Mamas." The mamas in the picture are Oma Davis, Nettie Murl Cade, Marya Dean, Nixene Davis, Elouise Brewer, Izola Ellis, and Katherine Carnes. Rosie Carnes Bussman and Dorothy Ellis McHam make their way to the Stillwater Farm Market Store nearly every day, and it is right on the spot where their mamas packed tomatoes in the summer.

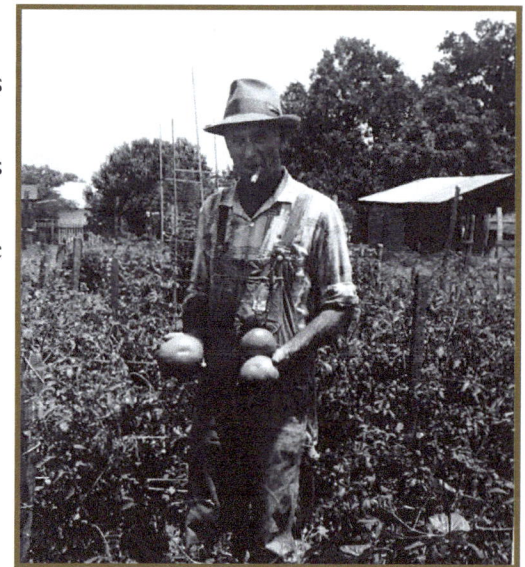

One more tomato story from my era. Mr. Johnnie Monk was a wonderful gardener who grew everything that a typical East Texas garden would bear. Mr. Johnny was known for several things, including his novel biscuit pan made in his shop out of sheet metal from car doors and hoods. He was famous, however, for his atypical tomatoes or 'maters, as he and

The Picklin' Parson's Cookbook

other Chandlerites might have called them back in the day. I remember on a summer Saturday he would come to Buford's barber shop, and I would be at my shine station. He would show off his 'maters to an admiring crowd, none more so than I. I have never seen a tomato—excuse me, 'mater— that large in my entire life, prior to or since. They were the size of large cantaloupes. He had a large, tan hand with cigar yellowing on his forefinger and thumb—from the King Edwards that he smoked most regularly—and one of his 'maters made for more than a handful.

What was the secret to his greener-than-usual thumb? Some say it was the heirloom seeds that he picked up from somewhere exotic years prior. Some say it was his touch; he just knew how to grow 'maters. I would imagine both to be true, but planting those tomatoes in the chicken yard had much to do with the success of his 'mater growing. Several inches worth of composted chicken manure—seasoning there for years—mixed with good ol' East Texas sandy loam soil made a perfect bed for a tomato plant. It took quite a strong tomato vine to hold such a massive fruit—or is it a vegetable?

There is that age-old question: Is a tomato a fruit or a vegetable? Botanically speaking, the tomato is a fruit. It contains the seeds of a plant. It is the mature ovary produced after a flower is pollinated. Therefore—according to the botanical definition—tomatoes, peppers, eggplants, and squash are fruits. Legally, according to laws passed by the U.S. Congress, it is a vegetable. In the culinary world, it is most often treated as a vegetable because it is served as part of the main meal, rather than as dessert. Around these parts we're just glad that Congress seems to have gotten one thing right. No one there considers a tomato a fruit. Perhaps it is the most versatile of all summer veggies, for it can find its way to the table as chow-chow, slang-jang, juiced for breakfast, fried up green for dinner, or sliced on a plate. One could also make a tomato sandwich, nothing else was needed but a little bread, mayonnaise, salt and pepper. And if you ask Mr. Johnny how he likes his 'maters, he'd say, "Boy, I sure do like 'em."

One might ask what ever happened to the culls at the tomato sheds that were set aside. Believe me, nothing went to waste. The culls would have ended up on the kitchen table in some form or fashion or made into tomato juice, relish or salsa. If you make some salsa, give thanks for the tomato packin' mamas and papas for the history, Mr. Johnny for the inspiration, and the chickens for the spat.

The Picklin' Parson's Cookbook

About the Recipes

In the cookbook we feature Tomato Shed Salsa (mild). If one likes it hotter, just add more pepper seeds. The salsa recipe calls for a rich blend of tomatoes and other delicious veggies. And speaking of veggies, Aunt Rose Cade is the inspiration of the Marinated Veggie Medley. If I listen closely, I can hear her voice as she lines out the instructions and creates her delicious veggie dish. Can you hear her? *"I like to serve this with peeled, chilled, fresh tomato slices with fried chicken and buttered new potatoes with their skins on for supper."* Wonder what she would say if I told her that Tammy entered the State Fair of Texas this year with a canned version of her veggie delight and won a BLUE RIBBON.

The Picklin' Parson's Cookbook

7
TOMATO SHED SALSA

Ingredients

- 20 medium ripe tomatoes
- 1 ½ c. white vinegar
- ¼ c. lemon juice
- 3 c. onions, chopped
- 1 ½ c. jalapenos (with seeds)
- 1 c. jalapenos (without seeds)
- 3 bell peppers (1 green, 1 yellow, 1 red)
- 6 Serrano peppers (more seeds make the salsa hot)
- 1 12-oz. can tomato paste
- ¼ c. kosher salt
- 3 Tbsp. sugar
- 3 Tbsp. Lawry's coarse ground garlic

Readying

Preheat the oven to 225 degrees, and place the canning jars right-side up on a baking sheet. Place them in the oven to keep them hot. Wash all of the vegetables—tomatoes, onions and peppers. Bring a large pot of water to a boil, and put the tomatoes in the boiling water for 1 minute. Remove tomatoes from the boiling water, and place them in ice cold water. Peel each tomato; also peel the onions and dice into small pieces. Dice all peppers into small pieces. Mildly chop tomatoes in a blender, but do not fully liquify.

Cooking

Place the chopped soupy tomato mixture into a large cook pot. Add vinegar, lemon juice, onions, peppers, tomato paste, salt, sugar, and ground garlic to the pot. Bring to a boil, reduce heat to low, and cook the tomato mixture for 45 minutes, stirring regularly.

Filling & Canning

Remove from heat, and remove the jars from the oven on the baking sheet and place on the counter. Ladle and funnel the hot mixture into the jars, leaving ½-inch headspace. Make sure all air bubbles are out of the jars. Follow a standard water bath practice for canning and sealing by submerging each filled jar into the boiling water with the jar tongs to heat on a low boil for 15 minutes. The process should yield 12 pints or 6 quarts.

"Round up your cookin' items. Burpless cucumbers are best. If you use a mandolin slicer, be very careful, and don't cut your finger off.

You can put the black pepper on at the table. I go along with (Louisiana chef and humorist) Justin Wilson.

His advice about not adding pepper too early or especially not cooking with black pepper as he said, 'It'll just swole up and lose its taste' is where I stand."

~Aunt Rose Cade~

8
AUNT ROSE'S MARINATED VEGGIE MEDLEY

Ingredients

- 4 to 6 cucumbers
- 4 onions
- 8 radishes
- 6 carrots (2 orange, 2 purple, 2 yellow)
- 3 bell peppers (green, yellow, red)
- 1 c. water
- 1 c. distilled white vinegar
- ¼ c. light extra virgin olive oil
- ¼ c. balsamic vinegar
- ¼ c. sugar
- 2 tsp. kosher salt

Readying

Peel the cucumbers, onions, radishes, and carrots. Carefully slice into 1/16-inch slices with a mandolin slicer. Slice the bell peppers into 1-inch by ¼-inch pieces. Whisk the water, white vinegar, oil, balsamic vinegar, sugar, and salt together in a large bowl until very smooth. Add the very thinly sliced cucumbers, onions, radishes and carrots, along with the bell pepper pieces. With a large wooden spoon, keep bringing liquid over the veggies until they are well coated with the liquid mixture. Cover with foil and refrigerate for 2 hours. Preheat the oven to 225 degrees, and place the sterilized pint jars right-side up on a baking sheet. Place them in the oven to keep them hot.

Cooking

Place the veggies in a pot, and cook to hot but NOT boiling. Remove from heat, and remove the jars from the oven on the baking sheet. Not much cooking required.

The Picklin' Parson's Cookbook

Filling & Canning

Remove the pint jars from the oven on the baking sheet and place on the counter. Ladle and funnel the warm veggies into the hot pint jars and fill with the liquid, leaving ½ inch headspace. Make sure all air bubbles are out of the jar, and the liquid completely covers the veggies that are just below the headspace. Follow a standard water bath practice for canning and sealing by submerging each filled jar into the boiling water with the jar tongs to heat on a low boil for 15 minutes. The process should yield 10 pints or 5 quarts.

NOTE: Best served chilled.

A STORY
Crazy Grandma Pickup Pickers & Pears

My grandmother "Gran" Copeland was a redhead and as fiery—in a kind sort of way—as they come. She was one of the hardest working people I've ever known. She was a teacher by trade and a cook and canner by passion. She was rarely idle, always thinking of something that needed to be done, and she hated to see anything go to waste.

Her yard and back patch featured a big fig tree, but it was full of large pecan trees that were very productive. We grandchildren had a rope and board swing in the biggest of the trees and would swing and play all year, but as the fall came about into early winter, the trees would be full of plump, meaty, paper-shell pecans. There were Stuart, Burkett, and easy-cracking Mahan pecans in the trees, and we waited for the hull to die and open, revealing the brown nut full of delicious nuggets that would give rise to pies, candy and tasty snacks. The wind would bring some of the pecans to the ground, but we would thrash the trees with bamboo canes to also knock the ripe pecans to the ground. Gran would pay us a nickel a pound to pick them up, and she had red mesh bags to put them in. Each bag weighed 5 pounds and better yet, it meant two bits (a quarter) to us pickers. We'd pick and swing, swing and pick, thrash and play, play and thrash an autumn day away. All the while people would drive by on the main drag through town in front of Gran and Pawpaw's house and honk and wave as homefolk were accustomed to do.

Outside of her pecan tree-shaded yard, it was almost as if God had planted a garden that no human hand had to plant or till. It grew to our delight and was at our disposal. Gran disposed of nothing and saw one of her jobs as making sure we honored the Good Lord by picking God's garden and enjoying the bounty for which we would be thankful. In the spring, our waste-not, want-not grandmother would send us out to pick dewberries, wild plums, or to find the pokeweed around the cattle pens at Uncle John's dairy. We'd find and pick the large leaves for Gran and Lola Bell Dewberry to team up in the kitchen and make poke salad. Understand that the pokeweed leaves are poisonous. In the soul food tradition, one would boil the leaves once and pour off the juice. Then the limp, bright green leaves would be seasoned, a little slab of salt pork would be added, and the greens would be boiled again to make a succulent greens dish akin to spinach, with a pot likker that was tasty and better yet, it wouldn't kill you.

As summer rolled into a breaking autumn, Gran was looking for two things. First was wild muscadine grapes that grew on the farm. There was a big loblolly pine tree that had a huge muscadine vine that grew all over the tree. One could shake the vine and fill up a good-sized bucket, never leaving the shade of the tree. The other thing? It was pears from the trees her beloved father "Ras" had planted. She could use some help gathering the pears, but if she wasn't in a hurry as usual, she'd pick 'em herself—just as she had since she was a little girl.

The east entrance of the farm features an old pear grove that was planted by Grandpa Ras, Gran's father. The pear trees are an old variety of fall pears called Kieffer. The pears are hard, ruddy and rusty in color, sometimes with an orangish tint. They are delicious. My redheaded Gran loved the fall Kieffer pears, especially the ones lovingly planted by her daddy. They were like fall gold to her.

I can see her now, with her best friend and sister-in-law Nettie Murl "Mammy" Cade there in the pear grove. If there was anyone who could keep up with Gran—and then some—it was Mammy. They would've talked Bud, Mammy's youngest son and renowned cowboy, into driving them to the grove in his old red and white Ford pickup. She and Mammy would start pickin' on the ground level, reaching as high and as fast as they could. Then they would get Bud to drive them underneath the trees to pick from the bed of the truck. He would drive them from tree to tree. As the next tier of pears would be out of reach, they would climb on top of Bud's truck cab and pick from there—the highest point. Here were two ladies in their late sixties, standing on top of a pickup cab on their tiptoes picking pears. All the time Bud would be saying, "Damn it, Mama and Aunt Rachel, you're gonna cave in my cab. It wasn't made for two crazy ladies standin' and jumpin' up and down to pick a pear." He'd laugh. He was half-kidding of course, but popping the dents out of the cab of his old truck was not unusual after such a pear pickin'.

Gran loved fruit trees—fig, pecan, and peach were in her yard and the back patch behind their house. But there was something special about the pears at the farm that her Daddy—who died before she'd finished loving him—had planted. There was something about the hard and ruddy nature of the Kieffer pear that made them her favorite. The pears Gran and Mammy would put in mason jars were nothing short of country masterpieces. The fall reminds me of pears and my Gran, great aunt Mammy, cousin Bud Cade, and the taste of spiced goodness.

The Picklin' Parson's Cookbook

About the Recipes

Autumn is not complete without pickled and spiced jars of fruit. Thanksgiving would not be the same, for sure, without the clove and cinnamon spicy taste of a pickled pear or peach half. The next two recipes are fall classics: Ginger- Spiced Peppered Pears and Cinnamon-Spiced Peppered Peaches. Both won ribbons at the East Texas State Fair, third place for the pears, first place for the peaches. In 2020, the pears won a blue ribbon at the State Fair of Texas.

The Picklin' Parson's Cookbook

9
GINGER-SPICED PEPPERED PEARS

Ingredients

- 8 lbs. of pears (summer pears or fall pears)
- 4 c. of water
- 2 c. white vinegar
- 1 c. cider vinegar
- 8 c. white sugar
- 1 c. Karo syrup
- 2-inch ginger (peeled & sliced)
- 2 Tbsp. whole cloves
- 8 habanero peppers
- 8 serrano peppers

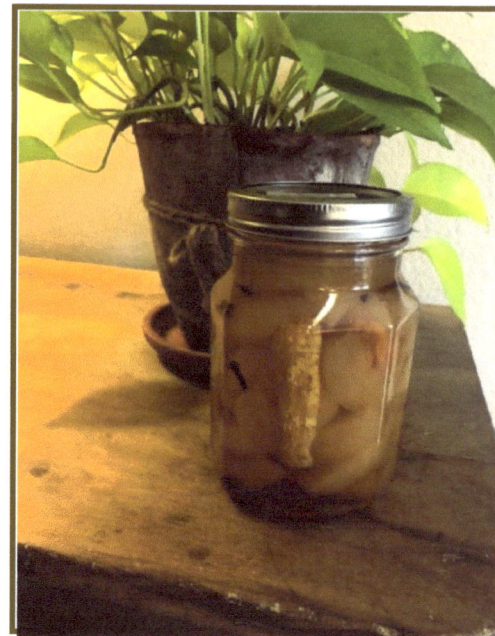

Readying

Preheat the oven to 225 degrees and place the sterilized pint jars right-side up on a baking sheet. Place them in the oven to keep them hot. Wash, peel, core, and quarter the pears and set them aside. With a gloved hand, cut the peppers in half and scrape the seeds out of the peppers and set the peppers aside.

Cooking

Combine sliced ginger (leaving 8 slices to put in the jars), cloves and a few pepper seeds—depending on how hot you want the pears. Put them in a coffee filter closed at the top, forming a "tea bag." Cheesecloth also can be used to make a filter. Combine the water, vinegar, sugar, Karo syrup, and spice bag in a medium-sized cooking pot. Bring to a boil, and then lower the heat. Let it simmer for 5 minutes, until the mixture is syrupy. Add a single layer of pears, cook until "slightly" tender. Repeat this step until all pears have been cooked.

Filling & Canning

Remove the pint jars from the oven on the baking sheet and place on the counter. Carefully pack prepared jars with pears and syrup mixture, adding a sliced piece of ginger, a piece of green (serrano) pepper and a piece of orange (habanero) pepper in each pint jar. Double the amounts for quart jars. Fill the pint jars with the hot liquid, leaving ½ inch of headspace. Make sure all air bubbles are out of the jar, and the liquid completely covers the pears that are just below the headspace. Follow a standard water bath practice for canning and sealing by submerging each filled jar into the boiling water with the jar tongs to boil on a low boil for 15 minutes. The process should yield 8 pints or 4 quarts.

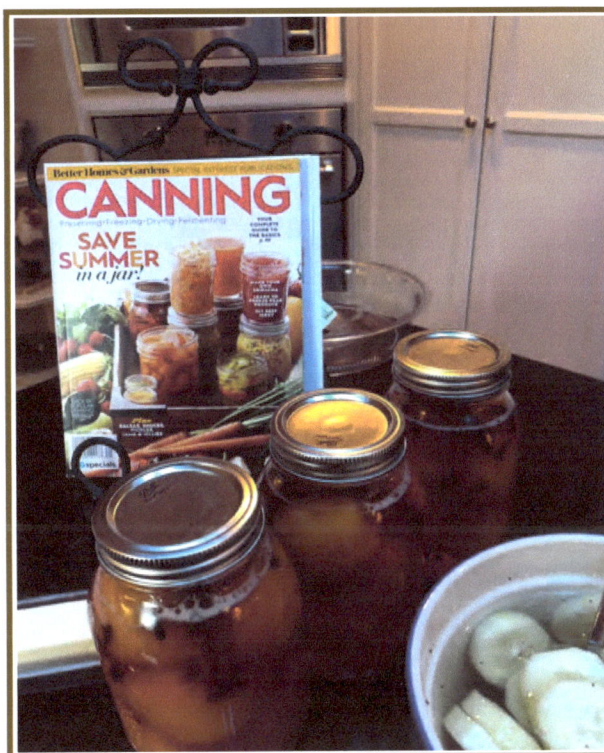

The Picklin' Parson's Cookbook

10
CINNAMON-SPICED PEPPERED PEACHES

Ingredients

- 8 lbs. peaches
- 4 c. water
- 4 c. distilled vinegar
- 7 c. white sugar
- 24 red chile de árbol peppers
- 8 serrano peppers
- 24 cinnamon sticks 2 Tbsp. Ceylon cinnamon
- 1 Tbsp. whole cloves
- ½ tsp. crushed red pepper per jar

Readying

Ready all ingredients in proper measurements. Bring a large pot of water to a boil; the canning pot can be used to blanch the peaches. Fill another large bowl with ice water. Wash the peaches and score cut an "X" into the bottom of each peach. Lower them on the rack into the boiling water and blanch them for one minute. Remove the peaches from the hot water, and immediately put them in the bowl of ice water. Once the peaches are cold, peel the peaches. The peeling will mostly come off by hand or a knife or peeler can be used on the clinging skin. Then twist, and the pit should be easy to discard. There is a cleave in each piece; cut the peach in half across the cleave—not with it. Preheat the oven to 225 degrees and place the sterilized pint jars right-side up on a baking sheet. Place them in the oven to keep them hot. With a gloved hand, cut the serrano peppers in half and scrape the seeds out of the peppers; set the peppers aside. Combine cloves and a few pepper seeds, depending on how hot you want the peaches, and put them in a coffee filter closed at the top, forming a "tea bag." Cheesecloth also can be used to make a filter.

Cooking

Combine the water, vinegar, sugar, Ceylon cinnamon, and spice bag in a cooking pot. Bring to a boil, and then lower the heat. Let it simmer for 5 minutes, until the mixture is syrupy. Add a single layer of peaches, cook until "slightly" tender. Repeat this step until all peaches have been cooked.

Filling & Canning

Remove the pint jars from the oven on the baking sheet and place on the counter. Carefully pack prepared pint jars with peaches and syrup mixture, adding 3 sticks of cinnamon, 3 red chile de árbol peppers and a sprinkling of cloves. Double the amounts for quart jars. Fill the pint jars with the hot liquid, leaving ½ inch headspace. Make sure all air bubbles are out of the jar, and the liquid completely covers the peaches that are just below the headspace. Follow a standard water bath practice for canning and sealing by submerging each filled jar into the boiling water with the jar tongs to boil on a low boil for 15 minutes. The process should yield 8 pints or 4 quarts.

The Picklin' Parson's Cookbook

The Picklin' Parson's Cookbook

A STORY
Baptists, Democrats, Damn Methodists & Beets

It is a political season as this cookbook is coming to be, and I had to add a splash of partisan flare. I think a person's brand of politics is somewhat inherited. Ask my Dad where he got his Democrat bent to politics, and he will partially credit his mom. Gran was a Kennedy—by way of Roosevelt—Democrat. Pawpaw Copeland, on the other hand, was a prim and proper staunch Republican businessman, always nicely dressed—whether in his druggist days or when he worked at the bank. I don't remember a lot of political conversations around their house, but I have heard my father state his political opinions that have increasingly become out of step with his neighbors. It's not that Dad never voted for a Republican. In fact, he confessed to voting for Nixon once; he just didn't like to do so.

My maternal grandfather Winston "Pops" Reagan, was a Democrat politician. He started driving a Greyhound bus when he was 18—some say 17—in part as his contribution to the war effort. He transported troops to their bases and citizens to their desired destinations. He retired from Greyhound after 40 years of service. But while he was driving across our county, he was readying himself for a run for county judge. My Pops never went even a day to college; he certainly didn't have a law degree. But he knew he would make a good judge, and that he did. After losing in his first attempt, he continued to drive the bus until he ran a second time. He beat the incumbent Democrat, and that was a day when Republicans in our county in East Texas were much more of a rarity than today. He never lost an election as an incumbent, and served 20 years as our county judge, hailing from the farthest point in the county, 23 miles from the county seat of Athens.

His father—my great-grandfather Samuel Oscar "Papa" Reagan—was a farmer, and he and Mama Reagan lived in a little white frame farmhouse most of their 73 years of marriage. Papa didn't have much of a formal education, but he was smart and wise and could spin a tale with the best of them. He was not just a Baptist. Papa was a Freewill Baptist, which as I understand in Chandler was a notch to the theological right of a regular old Baptist. His politics, however, did not match his conservatism regarding his brand of religion. I have his rocker in my office at the church, and many times I saw him rocking and smoking an unfiltered Camel cigarette as he quoted scripture and told funny stories. Sometimes, he would get quite serious and philosophical. He told me one day, "Stan, I'm a failure." "Why so Papa?" I said with a noticeable concern in my voice, which is what he was listening for with his exquisite timing. He continued, "I have

The Picklin' Parson's Cookbook

raised my seven kids to be two things. First, faithful to the Freewill Baptist Church, and second, to be loyal to the Democratic Party. And every one of them who hasn't become a Republican is a damn Methodist." Then he started laughing, squinting as he chuckled. He took another drag off the Camel, and looked at my wide-eyed expression. I didn't know quite how to handle Papa's humor.

Back in the day, I don't remember partisan politics being particularly "colored"—red or blue. I do remember the donkey and the elephant mascots. And I remember my family members who were Democrats, and those who leaned more to the right politically, Republicans. We all ate around the same table, and just didn't talk much about politics or anything that would threaten to ruin a good meal and conversation.

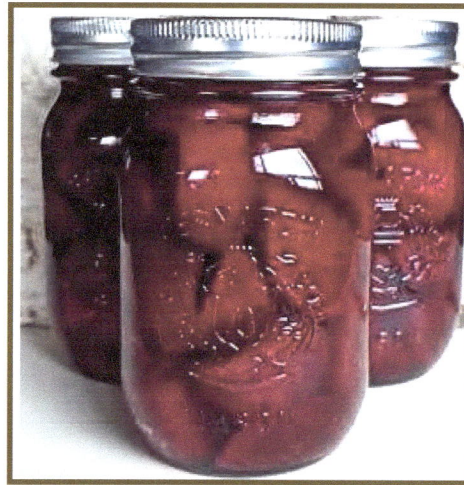

About the Recipe

I honor my dad, Don Cade Copeland, with this recipe. I wanted to feature one of his very favorite recipes, which is pickled beets. My father could eat bright red, pickled beets with every meal, including breakfast. He would eat pickled beets even if you told him only Republicans ate bright red pickled beets. He'd say, "Okay, then. I guess when it comes to beets, I lean a bit to the right."

The Picklin' Parson's Cookbook

11
REPUBLICAN-RED PICKLED BEETS

Ingredients

- 12 lbs. small to medium sized beets (golf ball to tennis ball size)
- 2 medium sweet onions
- 5 ½ c. distilled white vinegar
- 4 c. sugar
- 4 c. water
- 2 Tbsp. ground cinnamon
- 1 ½ Tbsp. salt
- 1 Tbsp. ground cloves
- 6 bay leaves

Readying

Preheat the oven to 225 degrees and place the sterilized pint jars right-side up on a baking sheet. Place them in the oven to keep them hot. Wash the beets, and cut the tops and the roots off.

Cooking

Place the beets in a large pot, and cover them with water. Bring to a boil, and then reduce the heat, cooking until tender. Remove the beets from the boiling water; put into a container of ice water for 30 minutes. Peel the beets, and cut into slices or chunks. Peel and slice the onions, creating rings. Bring the beet pieces to a boil in the pot with the vinegar, sugar, water, cinnamon, salt, bay leaves, onions, and cloves, stirring until the sugar and other ingredients are completely dissolved. Simmer for approximately 20 minutes.

Filling & Canning

Remove the pint jars from the oven on the baking sheet and place on the counter. Carefully pack prepared jars with beets and syrup mixture, adding a few onion rings to each jar. Fill the pint jars with the hot liquid, leaving ½ inch headspace. Make sure all air bubbles are out of the jar, and the liquid completely covers the beets that are just below the headspace. Follow a standard water bath practice for canning and sealing by submerging each filled jar into the boiling water with the jar tongs to boil on a low boil for 15 minutes.

BUTTERS, PRESERVES

(Yummm-Yummm)

JAMS & JELLIES

The Picklin' Parson's Cookbook

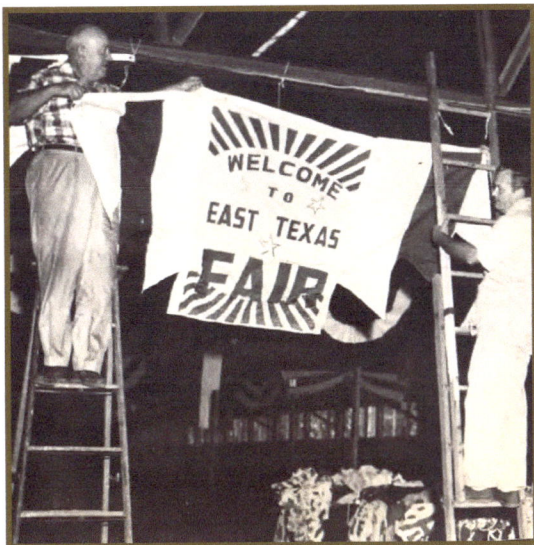

A STORY
Colored Ribbons, Candy Apples &
The Fair

I can still feel the adrenalin-enhanced excitement when the coming of fall would bring the East Texas Fair to Tyler, just 10 miles away from home. As a child growing up in Chandler, Texas, one of the big highlights of the year was going to Tyler to the East Texas State Fair. The rush of excitement was palpable, while staring at the "Hammer" ride and trying to convince myself to try that dizzying experience. To ride the rides and see the exhibits and farm animals created the excitement that was a true September treat. Eating a hamburger at the Chandler Lions Club booth was a must, but getting an apple covered with caramel or shiny red candy was the icing on an already wonderful cake that made the fair the "Fair!"

I even liked to watch as the candied apples were made. A wooden stick would be inserted into the sweet juicy apple. The apple would then be dipped and swirled until the milky, soft caramel or the sweet, sticky, red candy would cover the apple, sealing its goodness inside the essence of its sugary coat. Some caramel apples would be rolled in peanuts. The candy-covered apples would then be placed with another apple on the sheet pan. Some of the candy would also settle at the top and create a flat top of sorts for the apples. When I took the stick by the hand and held the apple upright for the first crunchy bite, all was good in my world. I lost a baby tooth once in a candy apple, and we never found it. But that's really too much information.

Last year, I entered my first jams and preserves in the East Texas State Fair. I had not entered anything to be judged since I was a youth in the Future Farmers of America or FFA, and that experience was not a great one. I had a shorthorn heifer that I fed every day, walked her like people walk dogs today, and shampooed and groomed her regularly. She was beautiful—at least she was to me. On the day of the judging, there was no other show heifer in her breed or in her age range. That's right, no other competitor! I quickly thought, this means I get a blue ribbon, and my heifer will be up for the judging as the Grand Champion Shorthorn—the perfect specimen of the breed. I could see the press surrounding me getting comments, "Stan, what has been your secret to having such a fine show heifer? What do you feed her? How often did you walk her, shampoo her, groom her?" Thoughts of grandeur filled my head.

The Picklin' Parson's Cookbook

The judge looked my heifer over very closely, and then picked up the microphone and announced that my heifer would get an honorable mention ribbon, because there were two heifers in the last class that were both superior to her. He made some other comments, but quite frankly I didn't even hear a word that the crazy—and obviously blind—judge said. I was embarrassed, and he was "dead" to me. My heifer was the only heifer in her class; therefore, she was the best in her class. Makes sense? Not to the judge apparently. So, needless to say, I was a bit gun-shy from entering any more East Texas State Fair contests with items walking and breathing or otherwise to be judged. But I had some good-looking and great tasting jams, preserves and pickled pears and peaches. What the heck? What's to lose?

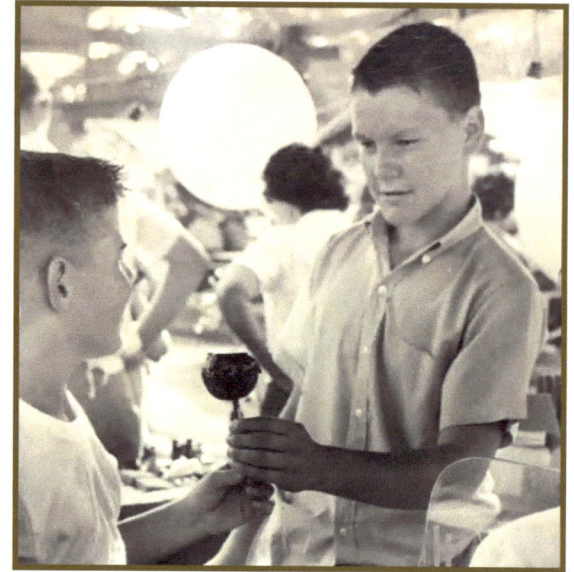

In 2019, my pickles, jams and preserves did really well at the East Texas Fair to my shock and surprise. The Pecan Praline Figs that received an "honorable mention" yellow ribbon at the State Fair of Texas—that is equivalent to a fourth-place ribbon—won a red second place ribbon at the East Texas State Fair. Mamma Hacy's Lemon Figs and Gran's Pear Honey won blue ribbons at the East Texas Fair. Cinnamon-Spiced Peppered Peaches also gained a second-place red ribbon, and the Moonshine Vanilla Peach Jam and Ginger-Spiced Peppered Pears both won third-place white ribbons. All in all, it felt a little like ribbon redemption.

Then came the State Fair of Texas in 2020. The Fair was closed, but the Creative Arts competition and canning was to go forward as planned. In fact, apparently more people were canning and pickling in quarantine than expected, and the entries were up over previous years. I had talked Tammy into participating with me, and she tried her hand at canning. We submitted our entries. Tammy won a blue first-place ribbon for her Aunt Rose's Marinated Veggie Medley, a white third-place ribbon for her Trinity Savory Pickled Okra, and a yellow honorable mention ribbon for Mamma Hacy's Lemon Fig Preserves.

My entries fared well too. I won blue first-place ribbons for my Garlic Pickled Okry and Ginger-Spiced Peppered Pears. I also received a red second-place ribbon for my Ol' Timey Pear Mincemeat. No ribbons for the Apple Butter, which is one of the most competitive categories, but there's always next year.

One of my favorite breakfast treats as an East Texas kid was toast and apple butter. Apple butter always reminded me a bit of applesauce, and what kid doesn't like applesauce? The difference in applesauce and apple butter is that the apples are pureed and smoother
The Picklin' Parson's Cookbook

in consistency, and also cooked longer to get a darker caramel color. The longer one cooks, the darker the butter gets. Well, my Caramel Apple Butter came up short at the State Fair and didn't win a ribbon of any color, but it tastes like I remember it tasted when I was a kid smearing it on my toast. Ribbons are nice, but you don't eat ribbons.

The Picklin' Parson's Cookbook

About the Recipes

I have created two apple butter recipes reminiscent of the East Texas State Fair. One is the classic caramel color apple butter, and the other is a candy apple butter that is red in color with a dark cherry flavor. Apples are not really an East Texas fruit that local farmers were ever known for. Typically, we look further north for the great apples we like to eat in Texas. However, more humidity-tolerant and hardy varieties have been developed lately. So, it is with fond memories and excitement that I share these apple butter recipes.

The Picklin' Parson's Cookbook

12
CARAMEL APPLE BUTTER

Ingredients

- 8 lbs. apples, peeled, cored and sliced (Envy, McIntosh, Gala preferred)
- 4 medium-sized Granny Smith apples peeled, cored and sliced (adding a tart flavor)
- 2 ¼ c. granulated sugar
- 2 ¼ c. packed light brown sugar
- 2 ½ c. apple cider (or apple juice)
- 2 ½ c. apple cider vinegar
- ½ c. lemon juice
- 1 ¼ Tbsp. vanilla bean paste
- 1Tbsp. ground cinnamon
- ½ Tbsp. ground cloves
- ½ Tbsp. allspice

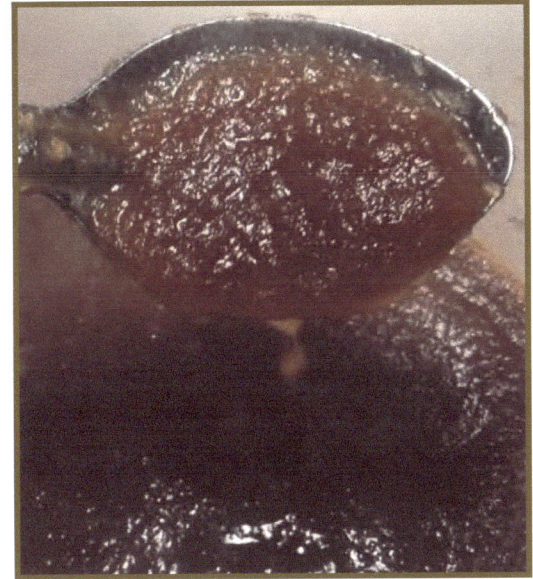

Readying

Preheat the oven to 225 degrees and place the sterilized half-pint jars right-side up on a baking sheet. Place them in the oven to keep them hot. Wash, peel, core, and slice apples—about 6 pieces per apple. Place the apples in a large pot with sugar, brown sugar, apple cider or apple juice, apple cider vinegar, and lemon juice; bring to a steady boil. Reduce the heat to medium and cook for 30 minutes; stir regularly until the apples are soft. Ladle apples and juice into a blender or food processor to puree the apples and ingredients until smooth and buttery.

Cooking

Return the puree to the pot, and stir in the remaining ingredients: vanilla, cinnamon, cloves, and allspice. Continue to cook on medium heat while stirring regularly for approximately one hour or until the caramel apple butter is the desired thickness. Turn off heat, and let mixture settle; skim any foam from the surface.

The Picklin' Parson's Cookbook

Filling & Canning

Remove the half-pint jars from the oven on the baking sheet and place on the counter. Ladle and funnel the hot butter into the jars, leaving ¼ inch headspace. Make sure all air bubbles are out of the jars. Follow a standard water bath practice for canning and sealing by submerging each filled jar into the boiling water with jar tongs to heat on a low boil for 15 minutes. The process should yield 10 half-pints or 5 pints.

The Picklin' Parson's Cookbook

13
CANDY APPLE BUTTER

Ingredients

- 8 lbs. apples, peeled, cored and sliced (Envy, McIntosh, Gala)
- 2 medium-sized Granny Smith apples peeled, cored and sliced (for tartness)
- 2 ¼ c. granulated sugar
- 2 ¼ c. packed light brown sugar
- 2 ½ c. apple cider (or apple juice)
- 2 ½ c. apple cider vinegar
- ½ c. lemon juice
- 2 boxes (3 oz.) dark cherry Jell-O
- 1 ¼ Tbsp. vanilla bean paste
- 1 Tbsp. ground cinnamon
- ½ Tbsp. ground cloves
- ½ Tbsp. allspice

Readying

Preheat the oven to 225 degrees and place the sterilized half-pint jars right-side up on a baking sheet. Place them in the oven to keep them hot. Wash, peel, core, and slice apples—about 6 pieces per apple. Place the apples in a large pot with sugar, brown sugar, apple cider or apple juice, apple cider vinegar, and lemon juice; bring to a steady boil. Reduce the heat to medium, and cook for 30 minutes; stir regularly until the apples are soft. Ladle apples and juice into a blender or food processor to puree the apples and ingredients until smooth and buttery.

Cooking

Return the puree to the pot, and stir in the remaining ingredients: cherry Jell-O, vanilla, cinnamon, cloves, and allspice. Continue to cook on medium heat while stirring regularly for approximately one hour or until the candy apple butter is the desired thickness and bright red color. Turn off heat, and let mixture settle; skim any foam from the surface.

The Picklin' Parson's Cookbook

Filling & Canning

Remove the half-pint jars from the oven on the baking sheet and place on the counter. Ladle and funnel the hot butter into the jars, leaving ¼ inch headspace. Make sure all air bubbles are out of the jars. Follow a standard water bath practice for canning and sealing by submerging each filled jar into the boiling water with the jar tongs to heat on a low boil for 15 minutes. The process should yield 10 half-pints or 5 pints.

The Picklin' Parson's Cookbook

A STORY
Christmas, Prolonged Family Feasts & Fruit

One of the very unusual gifts I have been given—and I know what a unique blessing it is compared to what many people experience—is extended family. Growing up around so many grandparents and cousins was simply a gift of grace. I knew two of my great-great grandmothers, three of my great-grandmothers, two of my great-grandfathers, and my maternal and paternal grandparents were very influential in my life. Add a wonderful Methodist church family with a town of loving Christian people, and the cup of blessing overflows. And then there was Christmas in the midst of all of it.

East Texas ways were fairly simple, but Christmas growing up was complicated. However, we kids really didn't know it. The spirit of Christmas was properly initiated with the setup of the live Nativity scene. We built the stable out of pine slabs provided by the local lumber yard. The characters were chosen, and bathrobed kids played the parts of Mary, Joseph, and the shepherds. The kings and angels had costumes. Then there were the featured animals. We always had a show calf, which was easy to get; and a donkey wasn't that hard a find either. No one in our parts had sheep, so goats always had to suffice. Never mind Jesus' parable about the sheep and the goats, goats were on the good side of the manger for our enactment.

Christmas with my family started on Christmas Eve. This was years before my life as a pastor would make this the busiest day of my year, and complicate it more. Conducting five Christmas Eve services right up to the eleven o'clock Christmas Eve Candlelight and a Holy Communion swan song has been my Christmas Eve experience for more than two decades. As a kid however, Christmas was a prolonged and progressive affair.

The Picklin' Parson's Cookbook

Christmas commenced with dinner—whenever we could arrive around sundown—at Mersie and Popsie Reagan's house. We would certainly open presents, but the big thing was the meal. It would be outstanding and vintage Mersie. She would have been planning and cooking parts of it all week, as she did hairdos for her faithful clientele that came to the beauty shop connected to the house. Dinner would feature an array of vegetables surrounding the moist turkey and dressing, and perfectly baked ham with delicious pineapple rings. The meal would be garnished with Virginia sweet chunk and bread & butter pickles that would make it to the table, as would spiced peaches and pears. A cake might be present, but pies were there for sure. Sweet potato, pumpkin, and pecan pies, along with perhaps a pear mincemeat featured for dessert. Mersie made sure the pear mincemeat was there for her favorite son-in-law, my dad. It was his mother's recipe, but in the country, cooking secrets were shared for all to enjoy. Pie would be served with freshly whipped cream—not ice cream, for we were not gluttons.

Then came Santa Claus on Christmas Day. Jolly Old St. Nicholas came to our house early, and we had to play with our toys quickly on Christmas morning because we had to be at Gran and Pawpaw Copeland's at 8:00 a.m. There was a little cooking to do, but it was well underway before we got there. A special treat on Christmas morning was chicken-fried quail, in a day when quail could still be found in the East Texas wild. Bacon, sausage, and country ham were also present because the quail would be quick to go. We had soft-scrambled eggs, hominy grits, toast, biscuits, and red-eye gravy. The gravy was a salty, sweet, dark brown liquid made from the grease of the country ham and day-old black coffee. It had just the right amount of salt. Sweetness infused the salty gravy with the addition of brown sugar or better yet ribbon cane syrup. My sister Jill and I didn't want to fill up on gravy when a fluffy buttered biscuit was begging for one of Gran's favorites or one of Pawpaw's delicacies.

One of Gran's favorites was one of our favorites too. It was fresh, homemade, pear honey preserves. The pears were picked off the trees at the farm not too many weeks prior to Christmas, and now they were sliced so thinly that you could nearly see through them in their preserved state. And they were as sweet as a pear could be. Each jar had two or three cherries in it, and getting a cherry in your dollop of preserves was like getting a prize in your Cracker Jacks. Uncle John and Aunt Vida (she was Dad's only sibling) were there with our first cousins, Cliff and Kristal. They were closer than cousins, since we were all so close in proximity and knit to our mutual grandparents. We kids sat in the kitchen, but we got waited on hand and foot. We were nearly too full to open our presents after breakfast, but we managed.

The Picklin' Parson's Cookbook

Following our time with the Copeland grandparents, we would drop in for an hour or so on Mama and Daddy Hacy. Our breakfast was settling, but our Ellis grandparents made us eat something too. Then it was off to Brownsboro to Mama and Papa Reagan's for a big country meal in a very little frame house. Mama and Papa had seven kids and a lot of them and their kids would show up for Christmas lunch and an afternoon of visiting. Hopefully, the weather was good enough for us kids to go outside and play. At the end of the day, I was tuckered out and filled to the brim due to nearly 24 hours of feasting and family fellowship. And Dad would end the day by unwrapping the extra piece of pear mincemeat pie that his mother-in-law made, sure that he got to end his complicated but blessed Christmas Day. The feast was really one of family—four great grandparents, four grandparents, a dozen or so aunts and uncles, and cousins galore. Santa Claus could barely wiggle in and find a place, but Baby Jesus was an invited guest in every table blessing.

About the Recipes

I guess when it comes to preserves and pies, our family really is partial to pears. The next two recipes are some of our favorite pear delights. And both of these recipes go back to my Copeland roots by way of our Gran, with a Lola Bell touch, of course. It doesn't get much better than Gran's Pear Honey on a fluffy, buttered biscuit. My Reagan grandmother's pear mincemeat that she liked to make was perfection too—in a pie crust to die for. The Pear Honey won a blue ribbon in the East Texas State Fair in 2019. The Pear Mincemeat won a second-place red ribbon in the State Fair of Texas in 2020.

The Picklin' Parson's Cookbook

14
GRAN'S PEAR HONEY PRESERVES

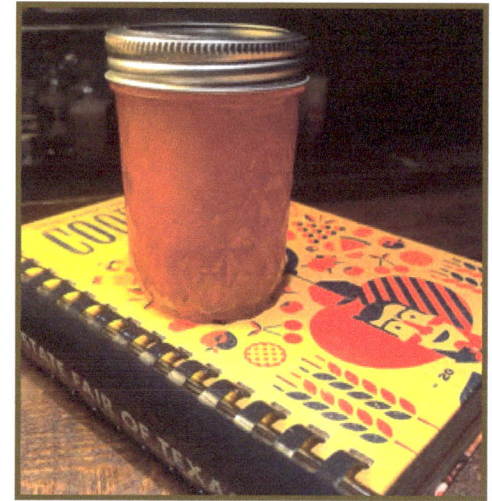

Ingredients

- 8 c. thinly sliced pears
- 20 oz. fresh crushed pineapple (canned crushed pineapple optional)
- 4 c. sugar
- ½ c. pure East Texas honey (or other local honey)
- ¼ c. lemon juice from fresh lemons
- ¼ c. fresh lime juice
- 1 8 oz. jar stemless Maraschino cherries (reserve 8 cherries, one for each jar)

Readying

Select firm pears; fall pears are wonderful, but firm pears of other varieties are fine. Peel and core the pears. Carefully slice them into thin pieces with a mandolin. Add the lemon juice, lime juice and sugar to the pears in a large mixing bowl. Mix well to make a "syrup" accompanying the pear slices.Refrigerate overnight, or for several hours, until the fruit is nicely chilled and beautifully white. It should have a nice sweet tartness, and it will get sweeter with the addition of the other ingredients and cooking. Preheat the oven to 225 degrees, and place the sterilized jars right-side up on a baking sheet. Place them in the oven.

Cooking

Empty the pear mixture into a large cooking pot, and add the pineapple. Begin the cooking process on medium high heat, stirring occasionally and bringing the pear mixture to a boil. Add the honey, cherries (except for 8 reserved cherries), and cherry juice. Reduce heat to keep the mixture cooking at a nice, smooth simmer for approximately one hour or until the desired color and thickness is achieved, all the while stirring. An orange-pinkish color and a medium thick syrup with the pear slices looking almost transparent is perfect.

Filling & Canning

Remove the half-pint jars from the oven on the baking sheet, and place on the counter. Ladle and funnel the hot pears and syrup into the jars, leaving ¼ inch headspace. Make sure all air bubbles are out of the jars, and place a cherry on top. Follow a standard water bath practice for canning and sealing by submerging each filled jar into the boiling water with the jar tongs to heat on a low boil for 15 minutes.

The Picklin' Parson's Cookbook

15
OLD-FASHIONED PEAR MINCEMEAT

Ingredients

- 8 lbs. pears (Kieffer or firm summer pears)
- 3 oranges
- 3 lemons
- 1 lb. black seedless raisins
- 1 lb. golden seedless raisins
- 2 lbs. currants
- 3 c. granulated sugar
- 1 c. apple cider vinegar
- 1 Tbsp. ground cinnamon
- 1 Tbsp. ground cloves
- 1 Tbsp. allspice
- 1 Tbsp. nutmeg
- 1 stick butter

Readying

Preheat the oven to 225 degrees, and place the sterilized pint jars right-side up on a baking sheet. Place them in the oven to keep them hot. Wash, peel, core, and slice pears—about 6 pieces per pear. Wash the oranges and lemons, and cut into eight pieces per fruit, removing all the seeds. Combine the pears, oranges, lemons, raisins, and currants in the bowl. Put 2 cups of the mixed fruit at a time in a blender, and chop until all of the fruit is a jam-like consistency. Add a little water, if needed. Cover and refrigerate overnight or for several hours until nicely chilled.

Cooking

Place the fruit mixture in a cooking pot on medium heat, and mix in the sugar, vinegar, butter and spices; bring to a steady boil. Reduce the heat and cook for 30 minutes, stirring regularly until the mixture has the desired color and consistency. Turn off heat and let mixture settle; skim any foam from the surface.

Filling & Canning

Remove the pint jars from the oven on the baking sheet and place on the counter. Ladle the hot fruit mixture into the jars, leaving ½ inch headspace. Make sure all air bubbles are out of the jars. Follow a standard water bath practice for canning by submerging each filled jar into the boiling water with jar tongs. Heat on a low boil for 15 minutes. The process should yield 6 pints.

The Picklin' Parson's Cookbook

A STORY
Figs, a Family Secret—Shhhhhhhhh! & Syrup

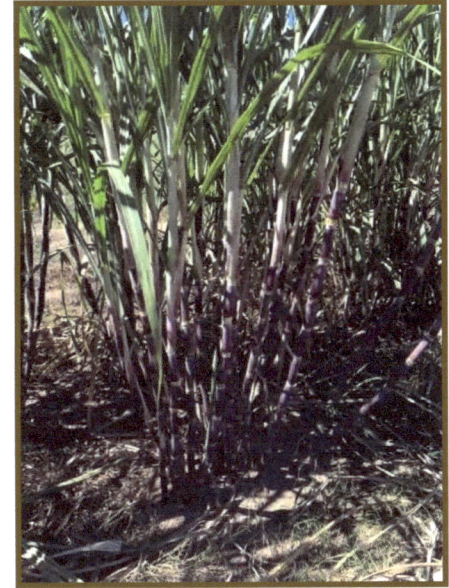

I know the keto diet is the latest food craze, and boy do I love meat. In fact, I have lost weight time and time again by eating a protein-rich diet, with the unnatural exclusion of carbs from my meals. I've probably lost 700 or 800 pounds eating that way, but will testify to the innate cravings for the sweet, sun-kissed, fruit of the land and eating the way God created humans without canine teeth to eat. As a picklin' parson, I yield often to the Good Book and the early promise of God bringing the people to a Promised Land flowing with dairy and carbs (milk and honey). And the Bible heralds the staples of grains and the fineness of pomegranates, dates, grapes, and figs. In addition, there was that feast resulting from killing the fatted calf, a feast reserved for a very special occasion. Also, there was Daniel who refused the meat of richness of the Babylonian palace and asked for a diet of nuts, fruit, and veggies. So, before we cast off a complete food group and go carb-free, let's lift up the fig and another secret ingredient to get at my Pawpaw Copeland's favorite biscuit topping delicacy. All things in moderation, of course.

One has to go back to an agrarian fall setting in order to fully appreciate the secret ingredient in the next featured fig recipes. The ingredient is "ribbon cane syrup." There, I said it. Ribbon cane is a particular variety of sugarcane. It doesn't have the greenish tint that the Louisiana cane has, and the taste of ribbon cane syrup is definitely not as strong as syrup made from sorghum grain. Ribbon cane grows a dark, rich, majestic purple in the field, and its taste is mild compared to sorghum or molasses. In a word, it's "perfection!" Figs really do benefit from the accompaniment of such a perfect partner as ribbon cane syrup.

I will partner with Jim Sidney Powell in raising a little cane for you to ponder. Jim tells this story from our Fitzgerald family roots saying: *"In early November the East Texas air added a fresh crisp coolness to the nights. This caused the sugar content to rise in the sugar cane stalks. It was time for the Fitzgerald ribbon cane syrup mill to begin its yearly operation. Taylor Fitzgerald, a co-owner of the mill, was my uncle. The other owner, Jim Fitzgerald, was Uncle Taylor's brother and lived just across the red clay and gravel road from the mill. Syrup-making involved a method of converting juice from the ribbon cane stalks into a thick, sugary liquid. It was a special fall happening in*

The Picklin' Parson's Cookbook

the Chandler community. Their mill was a Henderson County landmark, and it attracted customers from miles around, including my family. Their syrup mill was the only one operating in the immediate Chandler area in the 1940s.

In the fall, the cane was harvested by hand, cutting the stalks off at the ground with a machete. After the harvest, the workers hauled the cane to the syrup mill, just south of Uncle Taylor's house. Next, men stripped the outer leaves from the stalks. They extracted sweet juice from the stalks by squeezing them in a mill or a press that was powered by a mule. Tethered to a fifteen-foot pole, the mule walked steadily around the press in a wide circle, turning a shaft that was attached to the press. The press threw the squeezed flat canes into a pile, beckoning us kids to play king of the mountain on it. We were careful to dodge the yellow jackets buzzing overhead that were attracted to the sweet cane juice.

Once the unappetizing-looking green juice was collected, a chute transported it to a large copper vat that measured three feet wide by ten or twelve feet long, resting on rock supports over a hot wood fire. Part of the Fitzgerald ritual was for visitors to reach down with a tin cup, sampling the sweet juice before it reached the cooking vat. They even let the kids dip a tree twig in, and taste it while it was cooking. The juice was slow-cooked in the vat over an intense heat. It simmered and cooked, forming a froth that contained a little pulp and small bits of trash that had to be skimmed off.

It was important for the correct temperature to be maintained, as the juice cooked down over three or four hours into a beautiful amber syrup. Constant stirring with a paddle prevented it from scorching. The syrup would be cloudy if it wasn't cooked long enough. If it was cooked too long, it burned. The mill's chief cooker—a man Uncle Taylor hired every year for this job—was well trained in this skill, using his past experience, knowledge and sense of smell to guide him during the cooking process. When he sensed the syrup was reaching its right consistency, he dipped a wooden stick into the liquid. When the syrup ran off the stick in a string, he knew it was done.

Sometimes my Aunt Jewel, Uncle Taylor's wife, and Miss Ione—Mr. Jim's wife—made hot biscuits for guests to dip and sop the warm syrup. I enjoyed turning the biscuit on its side, poking a hole in it with my finger and pouring the fresh ribbon cane syrup into the cavity. I enjoyed every bite.

When the cooking process was completed, the syrup was drained out of the vat and into a huge cooling container. The syrup was then drained into shiny, half-gallon metal buckets with handles on them for transporting. Visitors enjoyed purchasing the syrup at the shed. Our
The Picklin' Parson's Cookbook

family went home proud owners of a couple of buckets of Fitzgerald ribbon cane syrup. Mama also used the ribbon cane syrup in her pecan pies, cookies, syrup candy with pecans or peanuts, and my favorite, popcorn balls."

Now, back to my Pawpaw Copeland's favorite delicacy and his special Christmas treat with a less than eloquent name—"lick." Pawpaw was an apothecary by profession and loved to mix compounds in the drugstore. To see him make his famous "lick" was like watching a skilled druggist at his trade. He would pour a splotch of ribbon cane syrup on a cleaned spot of his plate. He would then drop a spoonful of real whipped cream on top and mix it into a light caramel-colored syrup. He would take a biscuit and cut it into pieces and with his fork; he would slather each biscuit with the syrup to create a tasty bite. We kids loved to mimic Pawpaw to make our own concoctions, which were all mere variations of lick.

The Picklin' Parson's Cookbook

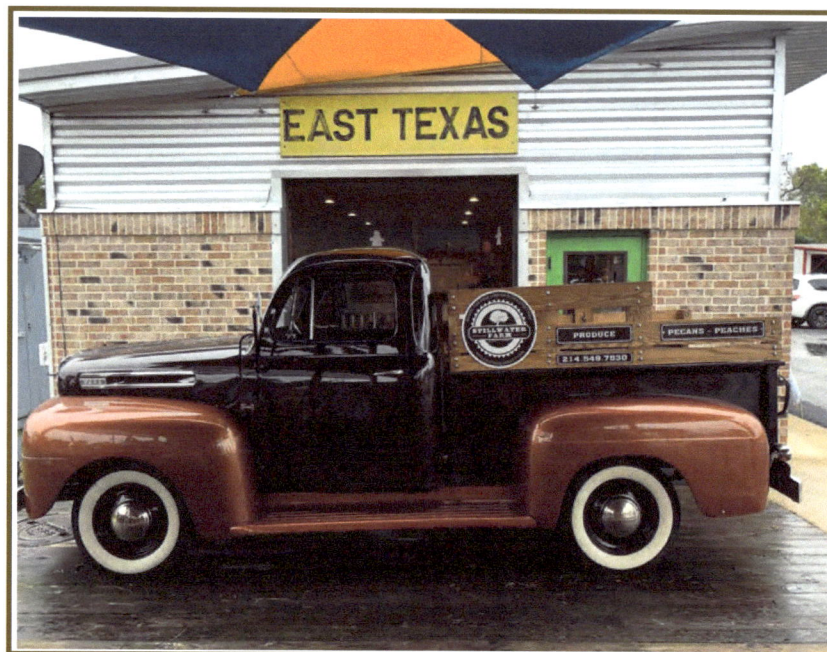

About the Recipes

The next two fig recipes call for a little ribbon cane syrup, and there is really no substitute. But if you don't have any, it would be best to add brown sugar rather than add a stronger-tasting sorghum or molasses. I think there is something special about the wedding of a fig to a little ribbon cane that makes the world a better place. I didn't enter the fig preserves in the State Fair of Texas competition in 2019, but I did enter the Pecan Praline Fig Jam, and the judges agreed it was worth an Honorable Mention ribbon. In 2019, I entered Mama Hacy's Lemon Fig Preserves in the East Texas State Fair and won a second-place red ribbon. Tammy entered the Lemon Fig Preserves in the State Fair in 2020, and they won an Honorable Mention.

The Picklin' Parson's Cookbook

16
MAMMA HACY'S LEMON FIG PRESERVES

Ingredients

- 8 c. ripe but firm figs
- 3 c. sugar
- 1 c. brown sugar
- ½ c. ribbon cane syrup
- ¼ c. freshly squeezed lemon juice
- 3 lemons, thinly sliced (reserve 20 slices to put in jars)
- baking soda
- 1 c. water

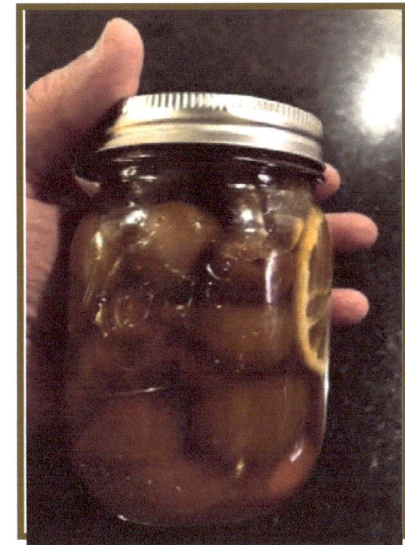

Readying

Wash the figs; prick each fig with a knife. Sprinkle them with baking soda; place them in a flat pan. Let them stand for 30 minutes. Rinse them gently twice, being careful not to mash or break the figs. Preheat the oven to 225 degrees, and place the sterilized jars right-side up on a baking sheet. Place them in the oven to keep them hot.

Cooking

Add sugar, water, syrup, lemon juice and lemon slices into a large cooking pot. Begin the cooking process on medium high heat, stirring occasionally. Add the figs carefully to the mixture. Bring the mixture and figs to a boil; reduce the heat to simmer and cook for 2 to 3 hours, stirring occasionally and gently. The longer they cook, the darker the syrup and figs will get. Cook to at least a golden-brown color. Turn off heat and let mixture settle; skim any foam from the surface.

Filling & Canning

Remove the pint jars from the oven on the baking sheet and place on the counter. Ladle the hot fruit mixture into the jars, leaving ½ inch headspace. Make sure all air bubbles are out of the jars. Follow a standard water bath practice for canning by submerging each filled jar into the boiling water with jar tongs. Heat on a low boil for 15 minutes. The process should yield 8 pints.

> And everyone else in Israel was of the same mind—"Make David king!" They were with David for three days of feasting celebration, with food and drink supplied by their families. Neighbors ranging from as far north as Issachar, Zebulun, and Naphtali arrived with donkeys, camels, mules, and oxen loaded down with food for the party: flour, fig cakes, raisin cakes, wine, oil, cattle, and sheep—joy in Israel! I Chronicles 12:39-40

17
PRALINE PECAN FIG JAM

Ingredients

- 8 c. ripe mashed Texas figs
- baking soda
- 5 c. raw sugar
- 2 c. brown sugar
- ½ c. ribbon cane syrup
- ¼ c. freshly squeezed lemon juice
- 1 Tbsp. vanilla bean paste
- 1 c. finely chopped praline candied pecans
- 2 boxes Sure Jell fruit pectin or liquid

Readying

Wash the figs; prick each fig with a knife. Sprinkle them with baking soda; place them in a flat pan. Let them stand for 30 minutes; then rinse them twice. Put the figs in a large bowl, and mash them with a potato masher. Pulverize praline pecans, and add very small pieces to the figs. Add lemon juice to the figs. Use a blender to mix them, but only for seconds—be careful not to puree. Refrigerate overnight or until the fruit is nicely chilled and beautifully dark in color with a light pink tint. Preheat the oven to 225 degrees, and place the sterilized jars right-side up on a baking sheet. Place them in the oven to keep them hot.

Cooking

Empty the mixture into a large cooking pot. Begin the cooking process on medium high heat, stirring occasionally. Bring the mixture to a boil, and reduce the heat to simmer. Add the sugar (raw and brown), vanilla, and ribbon cane syrup; cook for an additional 30 minutes or until it is a rich brown color and the desired texture. Add Sure Jell pectin in the last few minutes. Turn off heat, and let mixture settle. Skim any foam from the surface.

The Picklin' Parson's Cookbook

Filling & Canning

Remove the half-pint jars from the oven on the baking sheet and place on the counter. Ladle and funnel the hot mixture into the jars, leaving ¼ inch headspace. Make sure all air bubbles are out of the jars. Follow a standard water bath practice for canning and sealing by submerging each filled jar into the boiling water with jar tongs to heat on a low boil for 15 minutes. The process should yield 10 half-pints or 5 pints.

The Picklin' Parson's Cookbook

A STORY
"Green Like Me," "Cowabunga," & Figs

My wife Tammy and I have been blessed with two wonderful children—Zach who was born in 1986 and Emily who is a vintage 1992 model. Zach is an architect, as has been mentioned. He is married to Emily Schmidt Copeland, a pediatrician. They reside in Dallas, Texas with our first grandbaby Claire Marie (Claire Bear) and second that will be here before you read these words. Our daughter Emily is married to Jonathan "J.B." Bryant. Emily is a partner in a law firm in Dallas—Miller & Bryant, and J.B. is a United Methodist parson. We are proud of our kids, each and every one. I do want to tell this story about our son Zach when he was nearly four years old. And you need to know that in this family of many grandparents, he was the first-born grandson in Tammy's family and mine, and we thought then—and think now—that he is pretty special.

For the first seven years of our son Zachary's life, we lived in Houston. This was in the late 1980s, and Zachary was in love with the Teenage Mutant Ninja Turtles. Do you remember those little green guys? He had most of the figures. He watched the animated television shows featuring the activities of these green mutations. He even had a Ninja Turtle costume and would parade around as if he was one of his green heroes—Michelangelo, Leonardo, Donatello, and Rafael. He loved to shout their battle cry, "Cowabunga!"

I worked at the First United Methodist Church in downtown Houston. At the church, we had uniformed security guards who were not only good at what they did regarding security, but they also were very friendly and joyful. There was one young black man, Tommy, who was simply one of the best. He was friendly to everyone, and he loved Zach. Zach looked at him as a "hero" in his sharp dress uniform. One day Zach and Tammy had come downtown to see me at work. It was Monday, and I and the staff worked late on Mondays calling the visitors who had recently attended our church. It was good to see Zach and Tammy and visit with them for a while. Zach loved coming up to my office and working the staff crowd, ending up in Chester Steel's office for a few M&M's, but he also loved seeing Tommy when he came in and went out.

When it was time for them to ride the elevator to the ground floor, Tommy would be waiting on Zach and Tammy with a wonderful, friendly grin. He would then escort them to our car. I went down with them and was walking hand-in-hand with Tammy, as
The Picklin' Parson's Cookbook

Zach and Tommy walked hand-in-hand ahead of us. Zach was so proud to be with Tommy, but he was noticing their clasped hands like never before. I remember he looked up at Tommy, and he said with an odd concern in his voice, "Tommy, you're black." Tommy just chuckled and said, "I sure am Zach. And look at you, you're a nice color. Isn't it great that we are friends?" Zach said, "Yes." Tammy and I—who were still getting over our shock at Zach's question— noticed the puzzled look on his face.

I helped him get in his car seat, as Tommy looked on with that joyous smile. They pulled out, and Tommy said, "I sure love that little boy." I said, "Well obviously, he's crazy about you. And thanks for the care you take with him, and the good lesson you taught him today." Tommy just laughed and said, "I loved it." Shortly after I got back upstairs, Tammy called me and said, "While we were driving away Zachary started crying. He seemed to be so sad. So, I asked him, "Why are you crying?" He just whimpered. Then he said in jerky phrases, "It's Tommy, Mommy. It's Tommy." She said, "What about Tommy?" He said still whimpering, "Tommy is black, and I wanted him to be green like me." We both had a laugh at the innocence of his concern, as he really did think he was a Ninja Turtle and green as they were.

Later, I thought about the encounter. Though I celebrated Zach and Tommy's mutual love and appreciation of each other, it was the first time Zach had noticed their color differences. At least, it was the first time he talked about it. And their differences made him sad, as if he already sensed a separation now between the two of them. There seemed to be an innate longing for a homogenous connection regarding skin color. He was crying because one whom he loved was different than he was. He saw himself on an equal plane with his green superhero turtles, but he saw his skin color and his real, live, human buddy Tommy as a marked difference. It reminded me of my conversation in the lap of Lola Bell when I was about his age. We come to see the difference in skin color at an early age.

The Picklin' Parson's Cookbook

What we do with that difference, is the big question. If we come to internalize the feeling that having different skin colors is "just the way it is in God's beautiful flower garden" and can say and really celebrate the phrase "Isn't it great that we are friends?", then we have a chance to be pleasing to God, whose cherished creation we are. If we can truly be as Jesus said like "Blessed children, to whom belongs the Kingdom of God,'" then the world tends to be a better, more respectful, and understanding place. When little boys see law enforcement officers with their smiles and joy, it can forever change hearts. When officers see admiring children as ones they love and understand the depth of their influence on them, then we are not far from the Kingdom. In the end, it's all about relationships. A true relationship with God will always make us sensitive to others, respectful, seeking understanding, celebrating our differences, and rejoicing in our kinship.

About the Recipes

The next recipe is all about Zach. But I have found a place for it in honor of Tommy. Color had nothing to do with Zach's disdain for figs as a child. He just didn't like figs. No one in our family despised figs, so Zach's great-grandmother Mersie took it upon herself to make a masked fig jam that he would love. Mashed figs with strawberry Jell-O became transformed into a bright red, strawberry-mimicking, delightful jam. Our taste buds have changed, and we all like a little hot cinnamon kick with a cayenne topper. Zach still loves his figs this way. His favorite figs won a third-place white ribbon at the East Texas State Fair in 2019.

The Picklin' Parson's Cookbook

18
RED HOT FIG BERRY JAM

Ingredients

- 8 c. ripe mashed Texas figs
- baking soda
- 2 ½ c. sugar
- 1 c. water
- ½ c. ribbon cane syrup
- ¼ c. freshly squeezed lime juice
- 2 boxes strawberry Jello
- 5.5 oz. box original red hots
- 1 ½ Tbsp. Ceylon cinnamon
- ½ Tbsp. cayenne

Readying

Wash the figs; prick each fig with a knife. Sprinkle them with baking soda, and place them in a flat pan. Let them stand for 30 minutes; then, rinse them twice. Put the figs in a large bowl and mash them with a potato masher. Add lime juice to the figs. Use a blender to mix them, but only for seconds—being careful not to puree. Refrigerate overnight or until the fruit is nicely chilled and beautifully dark in color with a light pink tint. Preheat the oven to 225 degrees, and place the sterilized jars right-side up on a baking sheet. Place them in the oven to keep them hot.

Cooking

Empty the chilled fig mixture into a large cooking pot. Add the red hots, cinnamon, cayenne and water into the pan and bring to a simmering boil as you stir and melt the red hots for about 30 minutes. Add the sugar, ribbon cane syrup, and strawberry Jell-O. Cook for 15 more minutes or until it is the color and texture desired. Turn off heat, and let mixture settle. Skim foam from the surface with a spoon.

The Picklin' Parson's Cookbook

Filling & Canning

Remove the half-pint jars from the oven on the baking sheet and place on the counter. Ladle and funnel the hot mixture into the jars, leaving ¼ inch headspace. Make sure all air bubbles are out of the jars. Follow a standard water bath practice for canning and sealing by submerging each filled jar into the boiling water with jar tongs to heat on a low boil for 15 minutes. The process should yield 10 half-pints or 5 pints.

The Picklin' Parson's Cookbook

19
FIGBERRY BANANAS FOSTER JAM

Ingredients

- 8 c. ripe mashed Texas figs
- baking soda
- 4 bananas
- 2 ½ c. sugar
- 1 c. brown sugar
- ¼ c. freshly squeezed lime juice
- 1 c. water
- ½ c ribbon cane syrup
- 2 3-oz. boxes strawberry-banana Jello
- 2 Tbsp. imitation Jamaican rum flavoring

Readying

Wash the figs; prick each fig with a knife. Sprinkle them with baking soda; place them in a flat pan. Let them stand for 30 minutes; then, rinse them twice. Put the figs and bananas in a large bowl, and mash them with a potato masher. Add sugar, brown sugar, and lime juice. Use a blender to mix them, but only for seconds—be careful not to puree. Refrigerate overnight, (or for several hours, if you want to make the fig jam in one day), until the fruit is nicely chilled. It should have a nice sweet tartness. It will get sweeter with the addition of the other ingredients and cooking. Preheat the oven to 225 degrees, and place the sterilized jars right-side up on a baking sheet. Place them in the oven to keep them hot.

Cooking

Empty the chilled fig mixture into a large cooking pot. Add the syrup and water into the pan and bring to a simmering boil as you stir. Add the Jell-O and rum flavoring and cook for 15 more minutes or until it is the color and texture desired. Turn off heat, and let mixture settle; skim any foam from the surface with a metal spoon.

The Picklin' Parson's Cookbook

Filling & Canning

Remove the half-pint jars from the oven on the baking sheet, and place on the counter. Ladle and funnel the hot mixture into the jars, leaving ¼ inch headspace. Make sure all air bubbles are out of the jars. Follow a standard water bath practice for canning and sealing by submerging each filled jar into the boiling water with jar tongs to heat on a low boil for 15 minutes. The process should yield 10 half-pints.

The Picklin' Parson's Cookbook

A STORY
Mr. Jack Threw a Farmin' Cravin' on Me & Jam

Between 1900 and the devastating fire of 1921 that destroyed many of the buildings in town, Chandler was in its heyday, thriving with several manufacturing businesses. Sen. Ralph Yarborough said:

"When I was a small boy, Chandler had—in addition to two cotton gins and grist mills—two rather large industries. One was the canning factory; the other was a crate factory. At the crate factory, they took great logs from the large black gum trees cut in the forest. The wood was cut and put in a vat where the planks were steamed and swollen. Once they were swollen, they became impregnated with the steam and then were fastened to some kind of machinery and rolled over. Then thin slats were cut as they rolled, which—when dried—were manufactured into peach and tomato crates.

Peaches were canned at the canning factory. I remember seeing the cans with the colored labels on them, picturing large, beautiful Elberta peaches. I think it was called Chandler Canning Company. A number of Chandler young women from the leading families in town formerly worked there. I remember carrying lunch to my sister Orelia Yarborough (the third sister in our family) who sat at some kind of machine which fastened lids on the cans as they were filled with peaches. I remember seeing the machines lined up, and the young women, each sitting at an individual machine, and I remember the rattle of the machinery as the peaches were canned. I think Ophelia Cade sat next to my sister. They were two charming young women at that time. I would take my sister lunch, but I was rather awed by the noisy machinery and grown young ladies running it [the factory]."

The Picklin' Parson's Cookbook

For as long as I can remember I have loved to grow produce. Maybe it goes back to around the first of February every year when Daddy would get Mr. Jack Jackson to "break up" about a quarter of an acre of ground behind our house. To the east of the garden plot, Alice Ruth and Sam May had a little pecan orchard, and on the west side of the plot were two large mulberry trees that would bear the dark purple berries every year that mostly the birds greatly enjoyed. Between the trees was the garden plot that got plenty of sun and soil that Mr. Jack would turn up. It was light brown and moist. The freshly turned soil had a fragrance that was heavenly to me and memorable. You know how a smell can take you back.

Every time I smell freshly turned soil I go back. I can see in my mind's eye Mr. Jackson and his mule that was hitched to a Georgia Stock plow. Mr. Jack was a large black man, friendly and always had a ready chuckle to share as a response to my interest and ceaseless questions. He was up in years, but still plowing with his mule when I was a kid. The mule was tall and muscular, dark chocolate in color, with long ears and a lengthy blunted nose that was noticeably different than a typical horse. Jack called the mule "Ol' Brownie" as I recall, which was an appropriate name given the mule's beautiful color. Hearing the mule's name made me a little hungry for a chocolate treat.

Mr. Jack would walk behind Ol' Brownie as he held the handles of the plow and the reins to the mule in his right hand or sometimes between his teeth. When Mr. Jack would pop the reins and say, "Yipp," the mule would slowly start pulling the plow. The soil would start turning over, therefore, turning under the grass on top of the ground. When the mule would get to the end of the row, Mr. Jack would say, "Gee" to turn one way or "Haw" to turn the other way, and the mule would obey. Then Mr. Jack would say, "Whoa," and Ol' Brownie would stop so that the plow could be positioned again behind the mule and the plowing could resume. Soon another row would appear. When Mr. Jack was done and Ol' Brownie was loaded in the trailer, the patch was transformed into the garden again. We were so ready to plant it. I guess you could say Mr. Jack threw a farmin' cravin' on me that has lasted all of these years.

The Picklin' Parson's Cookbook

We would break the big plowed rows into softer soil with hoes and potato forks. The eyes of potatoes would be cut in slips of seed potatoes and little baby onion plants would be planted whole. We would soon plant tiny turnip and radish seeds in a very shallow furrow with just a sprinkling of soil on top. In just a few days, they would pop up to the surface and grow quickly to be the first thing harvested along with the potatoes. As it got warmer, we would hoe up little mounds to plant four or five squash or watermelon seeds atop each mound. Then we would wait several weeks for the delicious harvest. There would be peas and beans and okra and the rest in more standard rows that had been hoed and readied for the seed. We did have a secret ingredient that came from Uncle John's dairy, and there was a good supply—dried cow manure. This addition of the crumbly substance alongside the crops would turn the leaves darker green and cause them to really grow faster than normally they would. Every year we had a garden and perhaps that planted the farming seed in me.

When I was in high school, my friend Bill Pollard and I planted a peach orchard on our farm south of town that was the old Cade property, also once owned by my grandmother "Gran" Copeland, and we still own the land. Bill's family were nurserymen and came to own Texas Pecan Nursery Inc. in Chandler, which was one of largest bare root tree nurseries in the state. Texas Pecan Nursery—then as now—employs dozens of workers to do the hard work of year-round tree growing. Bill has come to be a third-generation nurseryman working this Pollard family business.

Bill and I lined out the orchard and planted the trees. Chandler's water and sewer works were adjacent to the property and spilled treated water from the sewer plant into a little holding pond that spilled over into a stream that eventually made it to Lake Palestine. We had a water pump in the pond that pumped water through six-inch pipes that were 20 feet long, and we linked them together to run up the hill to the orchard. In the orchard we had three-inch pipes that were 20 feet long, and each had a sprinkler head. We would move the pipes row by row after they had watered in place for several hours. The trees grew fast and beautiful in the East Texas sandy loam soil with plenty of water. Three years later, they were beautiful and in full production. The fruit was delicious.

The Picklin' Parson's Cookbook

About the Recipes

Many of the featured ingredients in this jam are grown on our family farm. We have peach and pecan trees that yield the very fruit used in the jam. And the whiskey, well we came by it honestly at the Turn Forks liquor store just south of town a few miles. A little shot of legal moonshine gives the vanilla a punch and adds flavor and aroma to bring the jam to perfection. And the preserves are as natural as they can be. I entered the Moonshine Vanilla Peach Jam in the East Texas State Fair in 2019, and it won a third-place ribbon. We might have won blue, but I presume the judges were Baptists like Papa Reagan.

The Picklin' Parson's Cookbook

20
MOONSHINE VANILLA PEACH JAM

Ingredients

- 8 c. ripe mashed Texas peaches
- 6 c. granulated sugar
- ¼ c. freshly squeezed lime juice
- 4 limes, sliced thinly for a slice in each jar
- 2 Tbsp. vanilla bean paste (or 2 Tbsp. vanilla extract)
- ¼ stick of butter
- 1 ½ c. whiskey bourbon or rye (divided in half)
- 1 c. chopped pecans
- 2 boxes of Sure Jell fruit pectin

Readying

Ready all ingredients in proper measurements. Bring a large pot of water to a boil; the canning pot can be used with the can rack for the peaches. Fill another large bowl with ice water. Wash the peaches, and score cut an "X" into the bottom of each peach. Lower them on the rack into the boiling water, and blanch them for one minute. Remove the peaches from the hot water, and immediately put them in the bowl of ice water. Once the peaches are cold, peel the peaches. The peeling will mostly come off by hand or a knife or peeler can be used on the clinging skin. Mash the peaches with a potato masher. Chop pecans into very small pieces. In a large mixing bowl, add the peaches, lime juice and sugar. Mix well, making a puree of mashed peaches. Refrigerate overnight, or for several hours, until the fruit is nicely chilled and a beautifully, bright peach color. It should have a nice, sweet tartness, and it will get sweeter with the addition of the other ingredients and cooking. Preheat the oven to 225 degrees, and place the sterilized jars right-side up on a baking sheet. Place them in the oven to keep them hot.

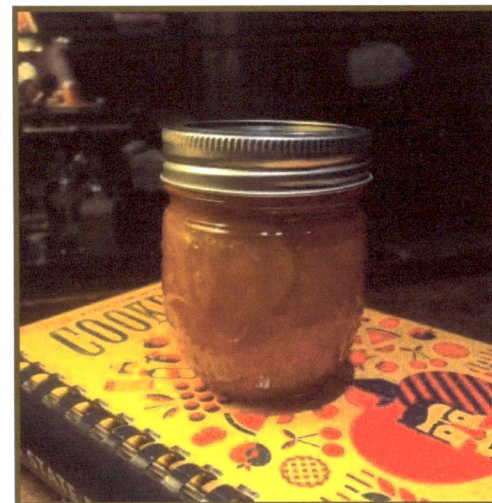

Cooking

Empty the chilled peach mixture into a large cooking pot. Bring the mixture to a boil on medium high heat, while stirring occasionally. Reduce the heat to a slow boil for about 20 minutes. Add the pectin, butter, vanilla bean paste, and pecans. Slice the limes, and add them to the mixture; also add half the whiskey. Cook for 10 more minutes or until the golden, peachy color and texture that is desired is reached. Turn off heat, and let mixture settle; add the other half of the whisky and stir it in. Skim any foam from the surface.

Filling & Canning

Remove the half-pint jars from the oven on the baking sheet and place on the counter. Ladle and funnel the hot mixture into the jars, leaving ¼ inch headspace. Put one lime slice in each jar. Make sure all air bubbles are out of the jars. Follow a standard water bath practice for canning and sealing by submerging each filled jar into the boiling water with jar tongs to heat on a low boil for 15 minutes. The process should yield 10 half-pints or 5 pints.

The Picklin' Parson's Cookbook

21
COUNTRY PEACH PRESERVES

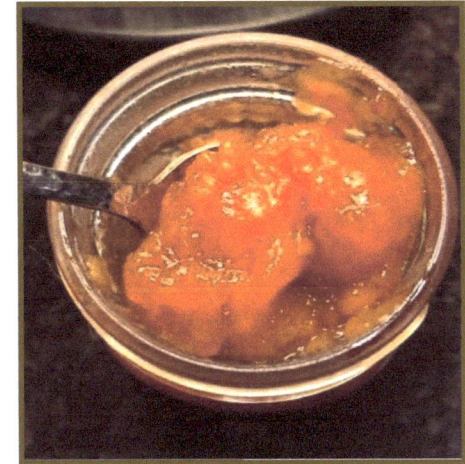

Ingredients

- 12 lbs. peaches
- 4 c. sugar
- Juice of 2 large lemons
- 2 Tbsp. cinnamon
- 10 cinnamon sticks

Readying

Ready all ingredients in proper measurements. Bring a large pot of water to a boil; the canning pot can be used with the can rack for the peaches. Fill another large bowl with ice water. Wash the peaches and score cut an "X" into the bottom of each peach. Lower them on the rack into the boiling water, and blanch them for one minute. Remove the peaches from the hot water, and immediately put them in the bowl of ice water. Once the peaches are cold, peel the peaches. The peeling will mostly come off by hand or a knife or peeler can be used on the clinging skin.

Thinly slice each peach, approximately ¼ to 1/2 inch, and remove the pit. If the peaches are nice and firm, a mandolin slicer can be carefully used. Place all of the sliced peaches in a large cooking pot, and squeeze in the lemon juice. Sprinkle well with 2 cups sugar, toss and sprinkle again with the remaining 2 cups of the sugar and cinnamon covering all the peaches. Let sit at room temperature for about 30 minutes or until sugar is dissolved. Preheat the oven to 225 degrees, and place the sterilized jars right-side up on a baking sheet. Place them in the oven to keep them hot.

Cooking

Place the uncovered pot on the stove, and bring it to a light boil, stirring occasionally to prevent scorching. Once the whole pot is at a light boil, simmer for 10 minutes. Let the pot stand uncovered until it is just warm to the touch or reaches room temperature. As soon as it cools, repeat the process of bringing the mixture to a boil, and then simmer. DO THIS 3 MORE TIMES, and if the process goes into Day 2, you can leave the peaches in the pot overnight without refrigerating them. The fifth time you bring the peaches to a boil and simmer, you will want to transfer them to the sterilized jars while still hot.

The Picklin' Parson's Cookbook

Filling & Canning

Remove the half-pint jars from the oven on the baking sheet and place on the counter. Ladle and funnel the hot mixture into the jars, leaving ¼ inch headspace. Put a cinnamon stick in each half-pint jar. Double the amounts for pint jars. Make sure all air bubbles are out of the jars. Follow a standard water bath practice for canning and sealing by submerging each filled jar into the boiling water with jar tongs to heat on a low boil for 15 minutes. The process should yield 10 half-pints or 5 pints.

The Picklin' Parson's Cookbook

A STORY
East Texas Blueberries, Politics & Jellies

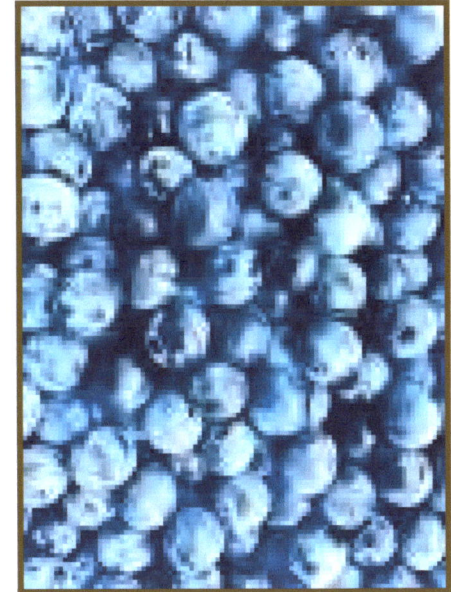

Blueberries when I was a boy were something we saw rarely because it was said that they grew "up north." Sometimes you could get them in cereal in dried form, but it just wasn't the same as a plump, round, juicy, sweet, little blueberry. Several decades ago, successful blueberry bushes that were tolerant of Texas heat and humidity were developed, and blueberries started springing up everywhere. Consequently, several large blueberry farms were developed in my home area that now are becoming well-known for delicious blueberries.

When one thinks about blueberries, pies perhaps first come to mind. A true East Texan may savor a blueberry fried pie. It doesn't get much better than sweet, sugary blueberries folded into pie pastry and fried—or baked if you like—to a golden brown. Unless of course, you had a big fluffy biscuit that you could drizzle with butter and then slap on a well-placed dollop of blueberry jelly.

Muscadines, on the other hand, grew wild on the vines connected to our many trees. To find a productive muscadine vine was like a jelly gold mine. It was important to beat the racoons, possums, and hogs to the berries when they hit the ground because they loved these native wild grapes with their tough hide and independent style of growth—no clusters. So, East Texas has always been muscadine territory and did not used to be blueberry-friendly, but times have changed.

2020 is a political year, and Henderson County in general—as well as Chandler in particular—used to be solidly Democrat or as we say today "blue." This connection probably goes all the way back to President Franklin Delano Roosevelt's New Deal. Chandler was marked with the work of the Works Progress Administration or WPA that was established with the President's executive order. President Roosevelt had insisted that the projects had to be costly in terms of labor, beneficial in the long term. The WPA was forbidden to compete with private enterprise, therefore, wages were kept smaller. The Works Progress Administration was created to return the unemployed to the workforce. The WPA built roads, bridges, reservoirs, and irrigation systems. The WPA employed more than 8.5 million workers who built 650,000 miles of highways and roads. The program also built 125,000 public buildings—hospitals, parks, playgrounds, and schools—including the school in Chandler.

The Picklin' Parson's Cookbook

The WPA built the school in Chandler with iron ore rock native to the area. The structure no longer stands as it did for nearly four decades. The rock wall still exists today and surrounds the new school building, serving as a reminder of a gift the town received from the government. The Rural Electrification Administration or REA used cooperatives to bring electricity to rural areas, many of which still operate. And of course, the crowning program Roosevelt signed into being was the Social Security Act on August 14, 1935.

In the 1930s there were few, if any, Chandlerites looking for communists or socialists in the midst of these government programs. There were, however, people throughout the country criticizing the government as being socialist through these programs and initiatives. Most knew those were desperate times demanding desperate measures, all brought on by the collapse of the economy and the markets on Black Thursday, October 24, 1929.

The highest percentage of rural people today are driven politically by promises of lower taxes, protection of guns, and more conservative approaches to hot-button social issues. Generally, less government involvement is attractive to most rural voters, unless it comes to needed stimulus checks or small business support—widely seen as needed right now. When all is said and done, we will likely add trillions to the national debt during this great recession. The debt would have been unfathomable to those in the days of the WPA, and it has grown immensely under the last three Presidents since Clinton, no matter what their political stripes. Both parties have their pet spending projects and have had financial challenges demanding response.

We have had three recessions in the last two decades, one brought about by 9-11, another severe recession brought about by irresponsible fiscal practices bringing on a mortgage crisis, and the other came to be this year ushered in by the tragic COVID-19 pandemic. In this time when unemployment is comparable to what it was in the Great Depression, we need political cooperation and more non-partisanship than we have grown accustomed to. We all hope this recession is corrected quickly—and as financially harmless as possible—with people returning to work in great numbers, as we saw in the last decade under both "blue" and "red" administrations. My hope is for the Red and the Blue, the Democrats and Republicans, to see fit to legislate together with more common goals than divisive elements being introduced into needed bills.

Sound like a pipe dream? What a great country we live in. Sometimes, I think within both parties there is a "Chicken Little caucus"
The Picklin' Parson's Cookbook

that claims the sky is falling if the other guys and gals win. I believe our great nation—which is a republic driven by the values of democracy—has been founded on principles that are bigger than any president or political party. The whole process should remind us that we exist as a nation FOR THE PEOPLE—<u>ALL</u> the people.

Here's something to ponder, how are we coming across to the young folks? My daughter Emily Grace Copeland Bryant is an inspiration to me. This twenty-eight-year-old millennial has always had a strong personality and a quick mind. She does her homework and knows the Constitution and the law. She knew when she was in high school that she wanted to be a lawyer. That was one thing, the other was that I had to quit telling lawyer jokes. Then she "swam the Red River" to go to Oklahoma University for her undergraduate work. I asked her, "What is your grandfather, the 'die-hard Longhorn' going to say?" She said, "Poppie will get over it." Then it was off to Texas Tech for law school. She married her college sweetheart, Jonathan Bryant "JB," and he is becoming a Methodist pastor. He credits his faith and "call to ministry" to my daughter, the lawyer, who is also a follower of Jesus.

She sees Jesus as a liberal and an activist for love. She is part of the generation of people nationwide that the church is finding it hard to reach, and the political parties are trying to bring them into their fold. She couldn't wait to vote. This year young people have voted like never before, and that is a good thing. She and her generation —which is definitely not politically monolithic—are by and large more open to diversity and more progressive on the hot-button sociopolitical issues than many of us Baby Boomers. She works with people who are not all of her political persuasion, but they are a firm—a partnership—and respect is a core value. What inspires me the most is her hope and belief in our country and commitment to make things better. Uncle Sam is in a pickle alright, and she knows it. But better days are coming, and she believes it. Furthermore, she is willing to work toward that end. She is fed up with the inability of our politicians and partisan citizens to work together. She doesn't "do" Facebook as faithfully as "old people" (her words). She makes fun of us who fight and say awful things to "friends" so that it feels like instigator friend is being heard. She is quick to point out that there usually is only a dozen or so like-minded people saying " Way to go!" and sharing "clapping" or "thumbs up" emojis. "What difference does that make?" she questions. I'm impressed with her generation, and we'll see how they lead us into the future. Plenty to ponder.

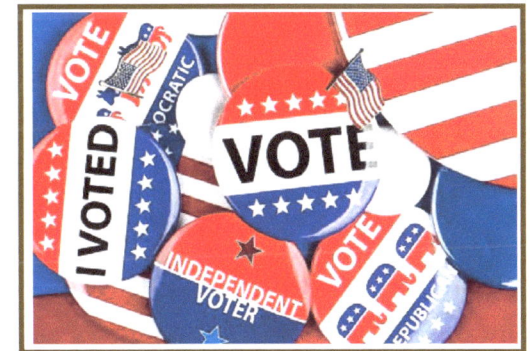

Bottom line, I think if we could get more Democrats eating my Republican-Red Pickled Beets and more Republicans eating my Democrat-Blue Blueberry Jelly, things would be better. So, pop the lid off the jars, pick up your favorite fork or spoon, lower your mask, and dig in. See what I'm talkin' about?

The Picklin' Parson's Cookbook

22
DEMOCRAT-BLUE BLUEBERRY JELLY

Ingredients

- 2 quarts fresh blueberries
- 4 c. water
- 12 c. sugar
- 2 pouches (3 oz. each) liquid pectin

Readying

Wash the blueberries thoroughly and remove the stems. It will be hard to remove most of them, but you can do it. Preheat the oven to 225 degrees, and place the sterilized jars right-side up on a baking sheet. Place them in the oven to keep them hot.

Cooking

Place blueberries in a pot with the 4 cups of water and bring them to a boil. While cooking them, you can crush them slightly with a potato masher, mashing occasionally as they cook. Reduce heat to medium, and cook them uncovered for 45 minutes. After cooking the blueberries, let them stand for 30 minutes. Line a strainer with four layers of cheesecloth and pour the juice back through the cheesecloth into a mixing bowl. Pour the juice back in the clean cooking pot, and heat on medium, gradually stirring in sugar until it dissolves. Then, bring the juice to a boil over medium heat, stirring constantly and stir in pectin. Continue to boil for 1 minute, stirring constantly. Remove the juice from the heat, and skim off the remaining foam.

Filling & Canning

Remove the half-pint jars from the oven on the baking sheet, and place on the counter. Ladle and funnel the hot liquid into the jars, leaving ¼ inch headspace. Make sure all air bubbles are out of the jars. Follow a standard water bath practice for canning and sealing by submerging each filled jar into the boiling water with jar tongs to heat on a low boil for 15 minutes. The process should yield 10 half-pints or 5 pints. Note: Muscadines, blackberries, or grapes can be substituted for the blueberries.

The Picklin' Parson's Cookbook

The Picklin' Parson's Cookbook

Award-Winning Recipes (Top Left to Bottom Right)

The Picklin' Parson's Cookbook

HAPPY ANNIVERSARY CHANDLER!

Celebrating 140 Years

of

Community & Commerce

1880-2020

The Picklin' Parson's Cookbook

"ALL" is the Key that Unlocks the Door

Pickling and canning is about "preserving" in order to later savor and enjoy, usually with family, friends, and community. This year Chandler is 140 years old. Human life and interactions in the area are much older. We do need to preserve our history, learn from it, repent of some of the wrongs revealed, but never let guilt and shame replace a real quest for reconciliation and "going on to perfection." And most of all, savor the best of what brings us together as a community, as a country.

May we always be thankful for those who have taken time to write histories and stories of Texas, Henderson County and Chandler that we draw heavily on in celebrating our collective life together. Given this year of 2020, I have attempted to bring forth some of the stories that at times are personal and some that needed to be told more widely in order to complete our real story of Chandler and its community and commerce. I see our history being like Pear Mincemeat. The mincemeat ingredients feature—along with the pears—the true flavor producers coming from the grinding, mixing, and cooking of oranges, lemons, raisins, and currants. When they are all blended together with the spices—cloves, cinnamon, nutmeg, ginger, and allspice—it is delightful to say the least. All spice? ALL is the key that unlocks the door. It takes the stories of ALL to make the story of ONE town, one country rich with purpose and meaning, learning and teaching, listening and caring, celebrating and being who God intends for us to be.

Heralded Son, Passionate Populist & U.S. Senator

One that stood among us—and had a reputation and practice of standing for all—was the Honorable Sen. Ralph Webster Yarborough, Chandler's heralded son. He is such a rarity compared to today's brand of politics. I hope we never fail to recognize the incredible gift we, as a community, have made to the larger nation through the senator and his service. The museum in town was his birthplace, and it was relocated in 2017 to the city park at the west entrance of town. Not too many cities—and virtually no small towns—can point to a three-term elected U.S. senator as being homegrown.

Sen. Yarborough stands as a politician of "days gone by," and it's easy for me to wish for more like him. "Ralph"—as he was enduringly called—was a stark contrast to most politicians of today that have for years contributed to our stalemated government. Ralph was a "people's politician" from a rural, working family in a river town in East Texas that he loved—Chandler. His main leg-up on the rest of us was not family wealth, instead it was his keen intellect,consummate people skills and rural roots that he knew how to leverage.. He was a statesman in a day when you could have disagreements with those within one's own party and even with those on the other side of

The Picklin' Parson's Cookbook

the aisle, and still go out to dinner. Table talk would be about the many things held in common, namely a love for country and commitment to make us better.

Ralph loved the working-class people and wanted the best in wages and education for all. He noticed inequalities and worked hard—even against those in his own party—when it came to needed changes through legislation. He served to move our great country to be a more perfect union, committed to freedom and justice for all. He was a patriot and a veteran. He was a Christian believer and loved God with his heart, MIND, soul, and strength. He was grounded by his rural upbringing in the best of ethical values and principles. His word was his commitment, and he could always be taken at his word. Because of caring nature, it was amazing that he was elected to the Senate and was re-elected once. Even then politicians like Ralph were becoming less preferred.

Perhaps more than anything else underscoring his ethics and commitments was his tireless work in the conflicted 1960s regarding race relations, for which he never got the credit that he deserved. This work of him championing and moving our country forward probably cost him his last Senate bid. He was constantly out of step with other Southern Democrats and enforcers of Jim Crow laws who stood firmly in place for segregation from the time of the Civil War. Ralph. He helped many other civil rights stalwarts in bringing down these restrictive and constitutional-ignoring laws in 1965. Now politicians like Ralph are "unicorns," and I do love unicorns.

Jim Sidney Powell's wrote about Sen. Yarborough in <u>Way Back When—Stories of Chandler's Past</u>:

Ralph Webster Yarborough was born in Chandler in 1903. He finished high school at Chandler High School and also at Tyler High, and later graduated with highest honors from The University of Texas Law School. He taught briefly at U.T. Law School, and practiced law in El Paso for three- and one-half years. He served as Assistant Attorney General of Texas for over three years and five years as Texas District Judge in Austin. He also volunteered and was commissioned as a Captain in the Army during World War II, serving on the staff of the 97th Infantry Division under General Eisenhower during the Crusade in Europe. In addition, he served in General George Patton's Third Army when Germany surrendered. He was redeployed and served a year in Japan under General Douglas MacArthur in military government.

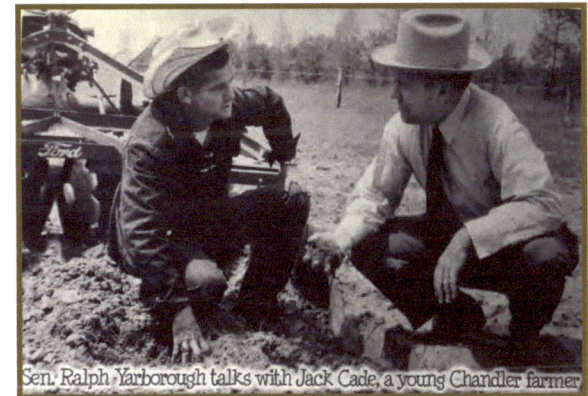
Sen. Ralph Yarborough talks with Jack Cade, a young Chandler farmer

The Picklin' Parson's Cookbook

Yarborough practiced law in Austin 1946—57 and ran unsuccessfully for Governor of Texas in 1952, '54 and '56. He was elected to the U.S. Senate in 1957 and then elected

to two more terms, serving thirteen years and eight months. He was a powerful political figure during those three terms, serving on the Senate Appropriations Committee and several other Senate committees.

While in the Senate, he authored several major pieces of legislation, including bills to create Padre Island and the Guadalupe Mountains National Parks and also led the fight for the Big Thicket National Preserve. In addition, he worked on bills enabling millions of students to attend college and expanded the Cold War GI Bill, enabling military veterans to attend college. During this time, he was named "Mr. Education of the Senate."

During his terms in the Senate, he passed more national legislation than any other senator from Texas at the time. He received many awards, medals, citations, honorary citizenship of counties and cities, and two honorary degrees.

Yarborough and his wife Opal had a son, Richard Warren Yarborough, who graduated from The University of Texas Law School. He married Ann McJimsey from a pioneer East Texas family."

What Chandlerites should never forget—and perhaps most proudly embrace— is that Ralph Yarborough was a legal and legislative force behind the scenes of the drafting of much of the civil rights legislation that was ratified and became the law of the land. It is no secret that President Lyndon B. Johnson and Sen. Yarborough—though in the same Democratic party—was not the best of friends and did not always see eye to eye. Yarborough was a supporter of Kennedy and often was the lone voice voting out of step with his "Old Confederacy" Southern Democrat colleagues. He was seen as a "liberal," though many would describe him as a "populist." A populist can be a Democrat or a Republican. A populist is a politician who strives to appeal to ordinary people who feel their concerns are disregarded by established elite groups, and most believe that was Ralph's driving credo. He would proudly say that he voted based on values that were planted in his heart from his upbringing in Chandler, his Christian faith and educated beliefs. He stood firm—and sometimes lonely—in saying we cannot dehumanize and dismiss whole races of people.

The Picklin' Parson's Cookbook

Texans & Native People

"ALL" causes us to see that before there were white immigrants longing for a place to live free or black slaves taken against their will and denied freedom, there were Native Americans. These people lived in tribes in harmony with the land and the bounty of it—game and fish, crops, wild vegetation, and clean fresh water. They were truly free, and there was a Great Spirit to whom they paid homage.

Pre-Chandler is a story of hope and sadness, of truth and lies, of life together and life too far apart to be bridged—due to sinful quests for homogenous living. 2020 has been a year of deadly pandemic and racial strife. To those who think we are in an era that is distinctively unique, know that some things are just simply slow to change. Pre-Chandler would have been a time when people died from diseases that are quite treatable today. We still struggle in the present day with that which has always diminished life and accepted some being treated as less than human. Chandler is near perfect to me, and my love for the town is great. People must, however, see their present reality in light of a past that is one of settlers, former slaves, and Native Americans. The Native Americans—sometimes called "Indians"—sadly, were those for whom a place could not be found among those so-called "settlers."

Joy Jones Clark wrote a history of Chandler for the book, *Chandler: Its History and People*. She wrote, *"Henderson County was created April 27, 1846; it extended from the Anderson County line northward to include part of the present counties of Kaufman, Van Zandt, Wood, Rains, and Rockwall. The eastern and western boundaries were the Trinity and Neches Rivers. When Van Zandt and Kaufman counties were created, it reduced Henderson County to its present boundaries with 946 square miles of territory.*

Chandler came to be located in the northeastern corner of Henderson county. It is roughly bounded on the north by the Van Zandt county line, on the east by the Neches River, on the south by Kickapoo Creek, and on the west by Kickapoo Creek and Battle Creek. The prehistoric inhabitants of this area were the Caddo Indians, later called 'Tejas.'

The earliest documented inhabitants of the area known as Chandler were Delaware, Cherokee and Kickapoo native people, according to Walter Prescott Webb's "Handbook of Texas, 1952." Both the Delaware and the Kickapoo belonged to Algonquin linguistic stock. In 1789 the Spanish allowed them to move into Missouri and into Kansas. In 1820, some seven hundred Delaware crossed the Sabine River into

Texas. The Kickapoo also migrated into East Texas at about this time. It was impossible to get an accurate count of these two tribes, as they were closely associated with the Cherokee Indians who migrated into East Texas around 1820. The Cherokee Indians claimed land in Texas along the Angelina, Neches, and Trinity Rivers.

A meeting of Texans at San Felipe in November 1835 called for the purpose of deciding Texas' position toward Mexico It recognized the danger of an unfriendly Indian tribe such as the Cherokee and passed a resolution of friendship with them, recognizing their claim to the land.

Chandler is some two miles west of this boundary, but they lived along the tributaries—now called Kickapoo Creek and Battle Creek—of the Neches River. There is said to have been Delaware villages along these creeks. The consulation from San Felipe asked Sam Houston, who had lived among the Cherokee Indians and had been married to a Cherokee, to meet with the chief of the tribe—"The Bowl," also known as Chief Bowles and Big Boles—to carry out this proposed treaty. Actually, there had been an earlier agreement on November 8, 1822, between the Indians and José Félix Trespalacios, governor of the province of Texas, which stated in part that the Cherokee could "cultivate their lands and sow their corps in the full peaceful possession." But in spite of this agreement, Chief Bowles decided to join the Texans in their fight against Mexico, hoping that this would assure them of legal title to their lands. Very little—if any—help was received by the Texans in their fight against Mexico, but at least the Cherokee remained peaceful during the Revolution. Just six months after the consultation at San Felipe, the war ended, and Texas had won its freedom from Mexico at the Battle of San Jacinto on April 21, 1836.

After the war, Sam Houston became president of the Republic of Texas. He did not turn his back on his Cherokee people, and he desired to live up to the agreement made before the Texas rebellion. Sam Houston told the Texas Senate on December 20, 1836, "I most earnestly recommend its ratification." In the Senate an Indian Committee found many things wrong with the treaty, and it was not validated. From this point on, the relationships between the whites and Indians deteriorated.

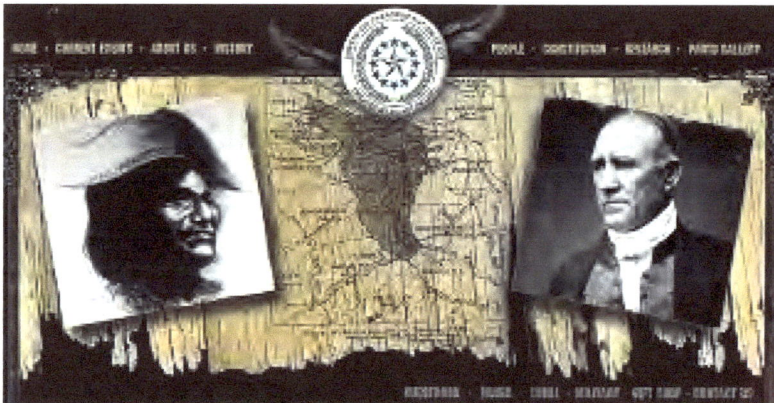
The Picklin' Parson's Cookbook

Dorman H. Winfrey in his writing The Battle of the Neches, states, "The main reason, however, why the Cherokee Indians had to be moved from East Texas was that there was not enough land for the Indians and the growing white population. The Cherokee Indians were accused of entering East Texas as intruders without a valid claim to any land."

When Mirabeau B. Lamar became president of the Republic of Texas on December 10, 1838, he made it very clear that he did not agree with Sam Houston on the Cherokee question and said that they would have to be removed from Texas. He said that he "was unable to think of the Indians except as an impediment to the progress of the white man." After several meetings between Chief Bowles and Martin Lacey, accompanied by John H. Reagan, no agreement could be reached between them.

"The Bowl" did not want to fight. He said that if he fought, the whites would kill him. He was 83 years old at the time. The prominent Texans who were sent by Lamar to talk with Chief Bowles were Vice President David G. Burnet and John H. Reagan.

On July 15, the Cherokees left their camp at the Neches Saline and marched west and north along the Neches. The Texans—with many prominent men in command of the various units—gave pursuit. General Thomas J. Rusk, Colonel Willis H. Landrum, General Edward Burleson, and Secretary of War Albert Sidney Johnson were under the command of General Kelsey H. Douglas.

Chief Bowles led his people to a place about two miles north of present-day Chandler and stationed his warriors along the banks of a creek bed now known as Battle Creek. He sent the women and children north. Dorman Winfred said that Chief Bowles had about eight hundred warriors. The Texans had split up, and so only about five hundred made the attack on the first day. The battle started late in the day, July 15, 1839, and lasted some two hours. The Indians lost eighteen dead and the Texans lost two. The Indians slipped away in the night and headed north.

The Picklin' Parson's Cookbook

On July 16, Generals Rusk and Burleson gave chase and found Chief Bowles and his warriors along the west bank of the Neches River. This battle site is on Harper Farm some two miles north of the Red Land Community. There was a very strongly fought battle between the Indians and the Texans. John H. Reagan's story of the battle tells us of Chief Bowles' appearance as he directed his warriors. Reagan said, 'Chief Bowles was a conspicuous figure. He was mounted on what we call a paint horse and had on a sword and sash, and military hat and silk vest, all of which had been given to him by General Sam Houston. Conspicuously mounted and dressed,

Chief Bowles rode up and down in the rear of his lines, very much exposed during the entire battle."

The Texans quickly gained the upper hand, and Chief Bowles was shot and killed on the battlefield. Dorman Winfrey said that "The Battle of the Neches climaxed a tragic episode in Texas Indian relations." The Indians were effectively expelled from the area, and it was now open for white settlement."

A "tragic episode" indeed, driven by much that was wrong and extremely regrettable. We must face our history, perhaps with a tear in our eye and a prayer of repentance on our lips. Would that Sam Houston's approach prevailed, which was to be "true to our word," "honor agreements," and "respect differences." General Houston believed the friendship forged with Chief Bowles and his people as the war with Mexico was escalating was one surely to be honored. Then, as now, politics sometimes trumps the best of human values, only to give way to fear and life-taking measures. In this case, actions were driven by racism, misogyny and greed for land for people who could find no place among them for the Cherokee people.

Community & Commerce

A lawyer and a student of history, Sen. Yarborough knew the treatment of the Cherokee people that gave rise to the white settlement of Chandler. He knew the plight of working-class people in general and the systems that worked against black people specifically. He valued the agrarian ways and the goodness of the land, and he fought for the respect of the environment. He was, of course, well-educated. However, he would say without exception, the greatest lessons he learned were from his upbringing in his beloved East Texas hometown of Chandler.

Sen. Yarborough contributed to the history of Chandler in the book *Chandler: Its History and People*. He wrote, "*I do not know who the first white settler in the Chandler area was. The Norwegians were the first white people to settle in that area of Texas. The contractor who sold them the land built a bunch of cabins on the bank of the Neches, and the Norwegians came there. A trapper was trapping up the Neches and told them if they settled there, they would suffer from fever and diseases that he predicted,* The Picklin' Parson's Cookbook

probably malaria, perhaps more serious things; and they moved to the higher ground near the mountain at present-day Brownsboro. Some of them lived right up on the mountain at present-day Brownsboro. They got out of the 'fevers and argues' that were concomitant results of living in low, swampy land near the rivers at that time."

Joy Jones Clark continued in her history of Chandler for the book, *Chandler: Its History and People*, "The first record of a white family in the Chandler area is that of Alphonso H. Chandler and his wife, the former Mary A. Brooks, and their seven children. They came to this area in 1859 and settled about one mile north of present-day downtown Chandler. They lived on the old road leading from Athens to Tyler. He named the place Stillwater. In 1872, he began the operation of a general store at his farm home. The U.S. government issued a certificate for a post office on April 17, 1873. Mr. Chandler was the postmaster.

In the year 1880, the Cotton Belt railroad was being built through the area. Mr. Chandler was very interested in having this railroad go through or near his property, so he made the Texas and St. Louis Railway Company a gift of land, if they would establish a depot permanently on the property. The railroad company named the new town Chandler.

Mr. Chandler built a two-story brick building—after an earlier one was destroyed by fire—across the road from the depot. This building faced south and was at the corner of Broad and Main Streets. Mr. Chandler made his home on the second floor. This building also burned in 1921. Mr. Chandler owned all of the land on the northside of the railroad, and he divided it up into town lots. He named the streets and started selling and building a town.

The building of a town in Texas, in the United States, meant churches, a school, businesses, commerce, cemeteries, and valuing the First Amendment in the establishment of newspapers.

Sen. Yarborough wrote again about his beloved town,

The Picklin' Parson's Cookbook

"The first newspaper in Chandler was the Chandler Times, edited by D.F. Hamilton. My brother, Harvey J. Yarborough, edited it for a while after D.F. Hamilton left. Mr. R. T. Craig of Paducah, Kentucky then bought the Chandler Times and lived in Chandler for several years while editing the Times. Later, the Chandler Record began and competed with the Times in the early 1920s. Both papers were to fold, but another newspaper was printed in Chandler briefly about eight or ten years ago, and it is worthy of mention. The fact that Chandler has had at least three newspapers in its history actually printed in Chandler is worthy of mention as indicative of its importance.

Prior to WWI, Chandler had two banks, the first bank being the First State Bank, and the second being the Guaranty State Bank. Later, the two banks merged. During the rise of the East Texas oil boom, the majority ownership of the capital in the bank was owned in Athens, and the people there paid handsome dividends and bought the stock of all the Chandler residents, liquidating the bank in order to invest their money in the East Texas oil field, where fast fortunes were being made—in large part by outsiders to the area. Chandler has never had a bank failure. All of the banks existed through depressions and all. I think it is to the credit of the people of Chandler and fairly rare in comparison to other small towns."

Take note: The old packing sheds were supplied crates from the local crate factory, and the peaches that were not shipped west on the train were canned locally by Chandlerites—nd this was an unusual town of less than 500 in population. So, pickling and canning has been a part of commerce in Chandler for over 100 years. Remember that when the canner is boiling on the stove, and the jars are being sealed with peaches, pears, pickles, and preserves.

Black Settlers Built Chandler Too

The story of Chandler would be incomplete without acknowledging the black settlers who helped build this area's commerce and community. The migration to Texas and Chandler was made up of white people, as well as former slaves who were moving in from the Deep South after the Civil War left it devastated. There were also a few plantations in the area north of present-day Chandler that had slaves prior to the Civil War.

Lola Bell Dewberry, who was born in 1923, said that her great-great-grandparents "owned" a farm in Chandler, though she did not know their names. It sounds odd, but within black families the history is foggy regarding settlement in Texas post-Civil War. In all of the writing about Chandler history—even the stories related to the Cherokee-Texan battles—there is little written of the settlement of black families in the area. Post-slavery, "free" men and free women and children came to Texas for the opportunity to own land and a farm in hopes of a better life and a more prosperous future. Their stories are still told at family reunions and the annual Chandler Community Reunion.

The Picklin' Parson's Cookbook

Part of the reunion folklore is about a town that no longer exists that was north of Chandler and in the area where a plantation once stood. The southeastern Van Zandt county town was named Blaine, Texas. It was on the Old Chandler Road to Highway 64, also the road to the largely black community of Red Land. It is described in Texas history being thirty-three miles southeast of Canton. The Blaine post office was established in 1893 and discontinued in 1907. Blaine was one of the first towns in Texas that had a black post office manager, in the 1930s. A school for black children was established at the site by 1890 and reached an enrollment of seventeen in 1903. At its height, Blaine had a black Methodist church, but the community never appeared on state highway maps and had no recorded population estimates.

If you ask most of the longer-term citizens of Chandler where the cemetery is located, they will say "atop the hill up from [the] old Yarborough homeplace and parallel to the railroad tracks that run on the southside." If you ask black citizens of Chandler, they might say, "Off of Walton Road behind the apartments where the big oak trees stand tall and wide." A trip to the cemetery—where the big oak trees stand—will put you in the midst of headstones dominated by Wallaces, Simpsons, Beasleys, and Montgomerys.

Many of those families trace back to one woman named Susan Dennison Manning. Mrs. Manning was brought to Texas as a slave from Georgia to just north of Concord Baptist Church where there once was a plantation. She brought with her to Texas two children—who had the last name Griffin. Among the children she would bring into the world was one with the last name Warf, and then there were two whose names were Sims. One of the Sims children was a daughter named Laura. When Susan married Steve Manning, they had five children, and Laura took the name Manning. Laura Sims Manning married Mark Wallace.

They purchased a 150-acre tract of land on what is now called Redbud Road and settled in to raise a family of seven children—Walter, Joe, Albert, Matthew, Sam, Maggie, and Caroline. Each one stayed in the Henderson County area. Walter, the elder son, married Caroline Thomas and had seven children—Harlee, Hubert, Maurice, Otis, J.B., Walter, and Vera. There is a pattern here of

The Picklin' Parson's Cookbook

seven-children families—and mostly male children—which explains the many headstones with the proud name "Wallace."

Rev. Harlee Wallace was a parson and a really good carpenter. He reared six children in the Chandler area. Harlee married Alice Simpson on October 4, 1923. Their children are: Margaret Cecille, John Milton, Alice Ruth, Charlie Delorice, Edna Earl, and Wayland Dewayne. Harlee began his ministry in 1936. His first call was to Free Will Baptist Church in Anderson County at Tennessee Colony, Texas. He served there seven years. He was then called to St. Paul Baptist Church at Malakoff, Texas. He served there fourteen years. He came home to Chandler and served until his retirement as the pastor of Macedonia Baptist Church.

The Mt. Olive Christian Methodist Episcopal Church and the Macedonia Baptist Church congregations had separate buildings. Rev. Harlee Wallace pastored the Antioch Baptist Church about seven miles from Chandler and the Macedonia Baptist Church in Chandler. He preached at Macedonia on the first and third Sundays and the Mt. Olive Church would meet at Macedonia. The Mt. Olive CME church had several pastors during this time. The photo is of Rev. July and the Mt. Olive congregation; it shows many who were among the stalwart citizens of Chandler.

The Wallace descendants number in the hundreds. Rev. Wallace reported about his children in the little book *Chandler: Its History and People*, "John had one son, Margaret had two sons, John and Alice had one son, Charlie had two daughters, Edna had three sons, and Wayland had a son and a daughter." The stories from this extended family alone would be countless. I have zeroed in on one descendant of Harlee and Alice—John's son Milton, who is the sixth-generation grandson of Susan Manning and likewise, sixth-generation Henderson County Texan.

Milton Wallace shared with me, *"Our family has a rich heritage with a lot of unanswered questions. My preacher grandfather, Harlee Wallace was the*

The Picklin' Parson's Cookbook

storyteller of the family. And the matriarch of our family was Susan Dennison Manning. Her daughter *Laura Sims Manning Wallace was my great-great-grandmother. Laura was a strong personality and married to Mark Wallace whose presence and disappearance is more mysterious. I would describe my great-great-grandmother as the "Victoria Barkley" of Chandler. Like Mrs. Barkley of the old television show Big Valley, she had sons to raise and land to tend and farm. She also had to run "The Shack" which was a store off of Two Street in Chandler, where people gathered for a soda water, café food, candy, and music, always music. Laura ran The Shack until her death in 1942. Everybody affectionately called my great-great-grandmother 'Mo-Lar." My grandfather Harlee was very proud of her and so was my dad, John Wallace. I remember as a boy helping the old folks tear down the old shack in the late 1960s. It was a sad day, for The Shack played an important role in our community for decades. You could almost hear the voices and laughter of the past coming from that shack built on Two Street."*

There are not many families—black or white—like Milton Wallace's who can claim six generations in the Stillwater and Chandler area dating back to the mid-1800s. These families have rich histories that have largely been told in the form of stories and rehearsed at annual family reunions. These reunions focused on the cemetery and the ancestors now gone, but not forgotten. These families flourished when Chandler's times were good, and they hurt when Chandler's times were painful. All in all, it was about a community that felt separate at times and together at times.

Though Chandler has been in many ways more harmonious regarding race and its life together, its story is still one of segregation. The separation may be most vivid with its cemeteries, and that is "what it is." Now, both the Black and the white cemetery grounds are sacred. The churches—as in most towns across our country—are separate Black and white. The schools which were once segregated are no longer that way, and busing led to advances perhaps, but they were at a cost—especially to children and families who saw their schools closed and the pride therein shift to other loyalties.

Milton Wallace said, "*I remember when our school closed in May of 1964. I was a little boy, but I remember that we had two teachers. One of those teachers was my mother, Thelma Jackson Wallace.*

The Picklin' Parson's Cookbook

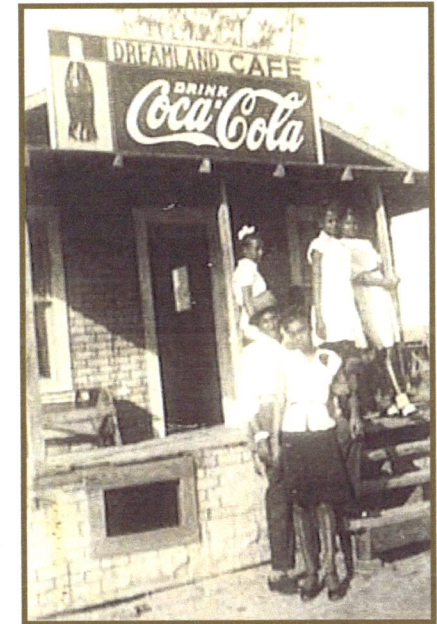

There was not a place made for her at the Chandler school with all of the turmoil going on surrounding the closing of our school and the integration of the white school. Mom got a job teaching in Terrell, Texas. That's when I moved with her to Terrell where we lived during the week, an hour away from Chandler and Dad. We returned to Chandler on the weekends where my father, John Wallace, stayed in our home and worked in Athens, Texas at the Curtis Mathes television manufacturer plant."

The closing of the Black and White schools, after they, in essence, were forced into a state of bankruptcy caused much unrest—addressed earlier in the book in the story "A Handful of Pickle and A Heart-full of Coach & Pickles." There were three votes taken as to which Independent School District Chandler Black and White children would go. A vote to be consolidated into Van's school district failed, as did the vote regarding going to Tyler. The vote also failed to be consolidated into Brownsboro, a smaller town seven miles away, but still in Henderson County. Finally, the State of Texas determined that Chandler would consolidate with the closest school in its proximity in Henderson County, and that was to Brownsboro. So, Chandler kids would go to school in Brownsboro. Chandler today is a town of more than 3,000 people, and all of the junior high and high school age students go to school in the neighboring town of Brownsboro that has a population of approximately 1,000.

Brownsboro's school made a place for Chandler students in 1965. The welcome was thorough and sincere. In 1965 and 1966, when the integrated Brownsboro Bears walked on to some East Texas football fields, opposing teams walked off the field refusing to play a team with Black players. In 1967, the "blue and gold" Brownsboro Bears—with Black and White players from Chandler, Moore's Station, Murchison and a few other little communities—won the 3A State Football Championship by beating El Campo 36 to 12. It wasn't even close!

When I went into the fourth grade, an all-Black school called Pleasant Ridge in Coffee City, Texas—approximately 12 miles from Chandler—was closed. Their students were bused to Chandler for elementary school and on to Brownsboro for junior high and high school. Moore's Station School was closed the year before with their students traveling approximately seven miles to Brownsboro. Busing was now the order of the day across the land. Starting in the seventh grade, for me, it was a seven-mile bus ride. For many of my Black friends, it was a longer, lonelier, tiring ride. These students were bused to Chandler where others would board the bus, then to Brownsboro—in total an approximate 20-mile bus ride. And, if the former Pleasant Ridge students participated in athletics, band, cheer squad, or other after-school activities, it was a later and more complicated busing experience. If we had an out-of-town basketball game on a Tuesday night, it was a very late return home and a very early rise to catch the bus on Wednesday. My early school experience with my friends taught me what my Black friends knew but rarely, if ever, brought up; our challenges were not equal.

We all became proud Brownsboro Bears, but did we adequately grieve what was lost regarding our communities—Chandler, Coffee City, and Moore's Station? Desegregation was needed, and yet it represented a massive change in thinking and living. I am so thankful for the experience of life together in school, in community and for those I call "friend." We learn more of God's ways the more we experience the beauty of the flower garden God created that Lola Bell Dewberry taught as she rocked me and sang the hymns of our mutual Christian faith.

Political Unrest Simmering but a "Pressure Cooker"?

So, what does pickling and canning have to do with the history of Chandler, and the larger 2020 picture in our country today? I have written this cookbook in the fall and in the midst of the 2020 elections. We have now elected a president and other national and state, county and city officials. We are also still confronting a pandemic that has ushered in a lifestyle that has us quarantining. Unemployment has become a reality for many; financially troubling times are looming. Today, racial strife has been the order of the day, and it has some of us fretting and others of us hopeful for advancement. In a word, Uncle Sam is in a "pickle." I encourage you to stop and do a little canning or enjoy the pickles shared with you by a friend, as you contemplate our plight in this country still experiencing the aftermath of the election.

Some might say we are in a "pressure cooker" right now in the good old USA, and it's about to explode and blow up. We—along with the whole world—have seen a Black man killed by the pressing knee of a policeman on his neck for almost nine minutes. We have seen peaceful protests being hijacked by violence, looting, and other criminal diversions. We have been subject to commercials of politicians bickering back and forth, offering few solutions and largely making a case for how the opponent is lying. Why? In part, because we've lost the true art of compromise or give and take i.e., all that makes this two-party system country really work. Let's not forget the democratic experiment that is the United States of America. It is held together by the checks and balances put in place by the Constitution and enforced by the Bill of Rights which ease the tension of the ideologies and parties. May we not fail to see the broader truth of our history, while celebrating and grieving appropriately.

We still argue about race regarding systems and structures. We see large companies and cities making moves that to some must feel like digression and for others, a sign of hope with healing in the air. We have seen sports teams and superstars call for change in the way we view race in our land and enforce laws. Confederate flags and statues have come down and are relocated; military forts, schools, and sports teams change their names or contemplate doing so. Are we really in a unique pressure cooker? Have we really never been here before? Maybe not exactly, but there have been some stark similarities.

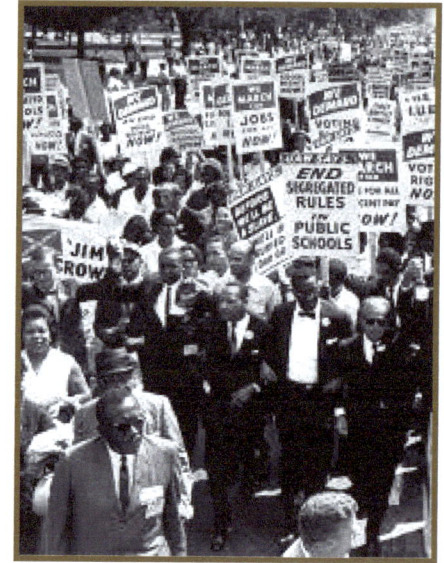

The Turbulent 1960s

May we consider the mid 1960s? A war was raging that we were losing, and young people were dying in a foreign land where we were also killing innocents who were described as "collateral damage." No one felt that was good. Bombing of Black children in their churches—along with lynching and dragging people to death outside their towns because of their skin color or their political activism—was a reality. Protests were everywhere, and slogans like "Burn baby burn!" were loud. As a country, we didn't know exactly how to get to a better place. Changes regarding race, like we had never seen before, were fast coming. Systems with which many were comfortable—and others were stifled by—were changing. But how many would make the necessary shifts? Women too sought more equality, and the sexual revolution joined the civil rights progression. Vice President Hubert Horatio Humphrey Jr. faced Vice President Richard Milhous Nixon in the post-LBJ presidential election. Then it was Sen. George McGovern vs. President Nixon a few years later. All of

The Picklin' Parson's Cookbook

this turbulence was followed by scandal, impeachment that was real, and fear of anarchy that never came.

The 1960s into the '70s was the time of my childhood in Chandler, Texas. Nixon, Humphrey, and even Wallace bumper stickers were on many cars. Schools were closing and busing was happening. Tyler's Robert E. Lee High School could no longer tout their mascot as being the "rebels," and the players would no longer run under the banner of the "stars and bars" flag, while the band jubilantly belted out "Dixie." Did we notice that we had gotten to the point that the few African American players on the "Rebels" team ran to the side of the flag, not stooping low enough to run under it? All was the order that became law of another Henderson County native, the Honorable Judge William Wayne Justice. He was despised by many fellow East Texans and heralded as a godsend by others. A pressure cooker? Did it blow, explode, or destroy? No!

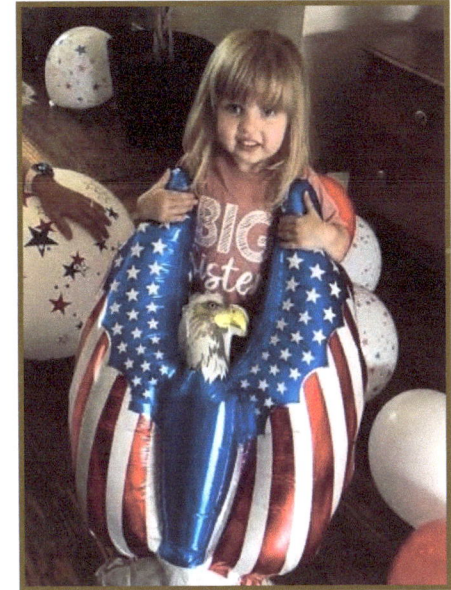

Like Water-Bath Canning Pear Mincemeat

It's hopeful to think that in this country—"sweet land of liberty" that we love, where every day we still fly Old Glory at the Stillwater Farm Market Store—we're going to be OK. We may be in a pickle, but from a picklin' parson you'd expect to hear, "Pickles can be good." Whether all stand tall before the flag in humble salute or bow down in silent protest, this is an odd time in our nation's history. We have to listen to the words and actions of one another to interpret the pain. We can also hope that we find a way forward that is full of mutual hope and thriving life together.

The Picklin' Parson's Cookbook

It is like we are in a water-bath canner, not a pressure cooker. Like the purpose of canning, I believe that no matter what, this land, our values and the essence that we love will be preserved and safe. The country will be able to withstand the elements that would otherwise spoil what is important—just like the purpose of canning and pickling.

Our nation and local governments exist amidst the sacred tension of our democracy. In the end, it's all just like canning pear mincemeat. This country is like getting citrus fruit together with the pears, raisins and currants. Then add the spice of cloves, cinnamon, nutmeg, and allspice. Mix it all together as the United States of America. Put the mixture in a jar, put a lid on it, and twist the band down tight. Bring it to a stirring boil for a little while. Let the jar cool off, and it will seal. Furthermore, it will be preserved and not spoil when confronted with the elements that seek to destroy it, making the consumer sick.

When you open the jar, be thankful for the goodness therein. Savor it as something passed down by generations through community. Share it with your friends, and even some enemies. That was the way Jesus did it. Get some more fruit or veggies, and start the process of picklin' and canning all over again. It's the way of life in the good old USA, and no people should know this better than those of us who have lived in rural America—especially proud East Texans and Chandlerites. I am so thankful to be a citizen of this great country and to count as my home and homefolk Chandler and its people.

God Bless America

While the storm clouds gather far across the
 sea, let us swear allegiance to a land that's free.
Let us all be grateful for a land so fair, as we
 raise our voices in a solemn prayer.

God bless America, land that I love.
Stand beside her and guide her
Through the night with a light from above.
From the mountains, to the prairies,
To the oceans, white with foam.
God bless America, my home sweet home.
God bless America, my home sweet home.

-- Irving Berlin

The Picklin' Parson's Cookbook

The Picklin' Parson's Cookbook

www.ingramcontent.com/pod-product-compliance
Lightning Source LLC
Chambersburg PA
CBHW040710150426

42811CB00061B/1807